HOW TO BE YOUR OWN SELFISH PIG

By Susan Schaeffer Macaulay

Illustrated by Slug Signorino

Chariot Books

ACKNOWLEDGMENTS:

Did you think that the person whose name appears as the author is the only one responsible for a book? In fact, special thanks is due for the hard work, creative energy, and help of a whole team.

Thanks to Sue Zitzman and Janet Thoma for their hard work in editing, and their friendship. To Ray Cioni for his creativity in graphic design, and Slug Signorino for his cartoons. To Franky Schaeffer V for his guidance and encouragement.

Thanks to my family: Margaret, Kirsteen, Fiona, and Ranald John. They gave honest opinions and even had to go without a few meals for this! Thanks to my husband, Ranald, for reading the manuscript constructively and helping with the research.

Thanks to Jerram Barrs for his theological check of the contents here presented. Last but not least, to Tim Zimmerman, Cissy Sights, Millie Thompson, and all the workers.

And how can I finish without a thank-you to my mother and father? Mother and dad, lots of these stories are yours. Thank you for you.

HOW TO BE YOUR OWN SELFISH PIG

First printing, July 1982
Second printing, January 1983

Produced in cooperation with Nims Communications

Edited by Susan Zitzman
Book design by Ray Cioni/The Cioni Artworks
Illustrations © 1982 Slug Signorino
Photos by Millie Thompson
Printed in the United States of America
Bible references, unless otherwise stated, from *The Holy Bible, New International Version*, © 1978 by New York International Bible Society, published by the Zondervan Corporation

ISBN: 0-89191-530-3
LC: 81-70769

Dedication

This book is dedicated
To some very good friends.
You'll know who you are
Because together we brought in the damp laundry
And put it in the "warming cupboard."
You helped chop all the vegetables
And stirred the porridge every morning.
I'll never forget you—
Your love, your help . . .
The fun and the laughter,
The music, and the talk.
Space separates us. Things happen.
But together we stand on firm ground.
There is life. We grow in truth.

Table of Contents

"What kind of a place is this?" — 9

1. "Don't ask questions." — 13
2. "As long as you're sincere . . ." — 21
3. "Let's all meditate on our navels." — 27
4. "I bet you believe in the tooth fairy, too." — 33
5. "You've gotta experience it yourself." — 39
6. "If it feels good, do it." — 49
7. "A bunch of fairy tales!" — 57
8. "You don't think anyone's going to hell, do you?" — 71
9. "That does not compute." — 81
10. "Defective merchandise: please discard." — 91
11. *How to Be Your Own Selfish Pig* — 101
12. "You only go round once in life, so . . ." — 113

Since I'm more used to talking with people than writing, I'd like you to imagine that this book isn't a book at all, but actually a visit to the rambling old house in England where I live along with my family and co-workers.

As you crunch up the driveway with your backpack slung over your shoulder, you will be welcomed by our dog, Timmy. His loud barks will announce your arrival.

If it is sunny and warm, you will soon find yourself sitting on the lawn, surrounded by thirty or so people. Some lounge back, soaking up the sun. Others are playing a game with five or six little boys. A few are gathered in a heated discussion. It is afternoon tea break, which is enjoyed for as long as possible in England.

But the people around you are not just from England or any one corner of the globe. Two young German students are talking with a couple of Americans. An Australian kicks the ball to the children, while four English students talk about their university courses with an older-looking couple. These people are dressed differently from each other, since they come from different backgrounds and countries.

Why is such a diverse group of people together? And where are you?

You're at a L'Abri Fellowship Center in a small English country village south of London. L'Abri (La-BREE) is a French name, meaning "the shelter." The L'Abri house I live and work in, like the other L'Abri houses around the world, is a shelter where people can come to get away from their everyday routines and think about their questions, and look at answers.

Some people come because of terrible personal problems: drugs, divorce, unwanted pregnancy, depression, suicidal feelings, alcoholism. Other people come just because they want to figure some things out. (The locations of the five L'Abri Fellowship Centers—in Switzerland, Holland, England,

Massachusetts, and Minnesota—do add some appeal to visits there, especially for people who like to travel!)

When I was fourteen years old, my parents, Francis and Edith Schaeffer, started the first L'Abri Center in Switzerland. It all began in 1955 when my sister Priscilla, the oldest of the four children in our family, went to the nearby university town of Lausanne, and started bringing a few friends home for weekends. These students were asking lots of important questions, which often led to one big topic: "What is life all about?" They couldn't believe that this family would sit and talk about their questions until midnight or 1:00 A.M. They loved the homey care my mother gave, the sled rides, and the family hot dog roasts. But what brought more and more young people to visit for longer and longer periods of time was the possibility of asking, thinking, and finding answers. My parents believed that you could talk about truth. They also believed that the roof over our heads and the food my mother prepared for those who came week by week would be provided by a God who was a part of our daily lives.

I couldn't even guess how many people have come and gone at L'Abri in the years since then. The original family grew up and had children of their own. Other people have come and worked in Switzerland and in the several other new L'Abri centers. The L'Abri you are visiting in England started eleven years ago.

In this book you'll share with me some stories of people's lives and their ideas. The questions and problems are real ones; the people who had them are real, too. (I changed some details to protect their privacy.)

Don't pack lots of fancy clothes when you come. Bring your very oldest jeans, and lots of warm sweaters. I'm afraid the huge, old manor house (built in 1789) gets chilly, and there's lots of work to do. Everyone is asked to help with the laundry, gardening, cooking, etc! You will study for four hours and help for four hours every day.

The people living and working here at L'Abri are my husband, Ranald, and myself, three of our four children (our oldest daughter is at college), plus three other families and three single workers. At mealtime, you may have a meal somewhere in the main house, in the old stable block, in an apartment, or in the old schoolhouse, all turned into homes of those working here. Upstairs there are bunk beds to flop down on at night. You will get very tired!

This visit will be easy to arrange. All you have to do is turn the page. Sometimes there are more people who want to come to L'Abri than we can house. But in this case, you can visit and eavesdrop without even writing a letter. I hope the ideas we discuss will jump the gap of the space that separates us. Come and join our conversations. They sometimes last for hours!

Sally sank into an armchair by the crackling fire and closed her hand around a cup of coffee. Traces of tears smudged her cheeks, and her hands shook. Her wrist, freshly bandaged where she had slashed it, made her wince whenever she moved.

As I sat down across from her, my heart sank. What should I say? I decided just to listen.

"My life is such a mess, . . ." Sally murmured, staring into the fire. "The whole world is a mess. And I don't think it's going to get better. What's the use in going on living?"

On another day Matthew stood by the kitchen sink, washing stacks of cups with short, jerky motions. It looked as if he were trying to kill the cups!

"Take a look at me!" he said. "People say I'm a success. Ha! If only they knew." He laughed bitterly. "I thought I had it made, too. I finished school, got an 'important' job, could afford a comfortable life-style, had a beautiful girl friend. I really cared about this girl, too, and the future looked promising. . . ." His voice trailed off.

"But then our feelings for each other died," he continued, getting angry again, "and we broke the thing up! I was miserable. And, you know, as I looked around at everything else that I had, it all tasted like—like sawdust without her."

He turned from the sink to glare at me. "What's this crummy life all about, anyway?"

Next time you're out with a friend for a hamburger and fries or a sundae, try to look your friend in the eye and ask Sally's or Matthew's questions: "What is life all about?" "What's the use in going on living?"

Your friend will very likely joke or laugh, not believing you're serious. Or he might stare at you nervously, or even call a psychiatrist. After all, people don't usually ask those

**"And yet they drink, they laugh;
Close the wound, hide the scar . . ."**

Carly Simon, "That's the Way I've Always Heard It Should Be"

kinds of questions. Our culture tends to squelch deep thinking, or else to label it as something that only superbrains or strange people do.

Yet Sally and Matthew aren't weird. They are real people I've known, two out of many who have brought their questions to L'Abri Fellowship in Greatham, England, where I live and work.

Why were they asking questions, when most people don't bother to? Because difficult events in their lives had shaken them cruelly. The way they'd tried living wasn't working. They'd come to the end of their rope.

Rather than weird, Sally and Matthew are quite typical. Have you ever noticed that people usually only pay attention to the "heavy questions" of life when things go wrong?

We don't do much serious examining of ourselves after getting a date with Mister or Miss Wonderful—but we do after that same person has informed us that he/she is shampooing his/her hair that night! We're less inclined to think deep thoughts after winning a championship game than after losing in a shutout.

When things in life are going along well, we assume that we must be doing something right. It's when they go wrong that we begin to wonder. And even then we often try to shut out the questions that bother us. We go to a party, or turn the music up louder, or work harder. We buy a new sweater or a pair of skis to cheer ourselves up, or drown our problems with a chocolate shake or a few beers or a few pills.

"Don't think about it," society tells us. "Don't ask questions."

You might say that the culture around us brainwashes us. There are more images and words thrown at us every day than ever before in man's history. Magazines, tv, newspapers: these form the media. They are out to sell opinions to us. On top of this, we are surrounded by friends and neighbors who tend to repeat what they have heard. Some people say that young people are especially susceptible to being influenced by their peers. That may be true. But everyone tends to think that the ideas most people have accepted must therefore be "right" ideas. We forget to think for ourselves.

But no one can run away from these questions and decisions forever. You already believe in something. Whether you've thought about it or not, you have your own philosophy of life. It's made up of what you believe about right and wrong, life and death, truth and God and man. And your life view affects you. It affects the way you take a test tomorrow as well as what you'll do in a job or in your love life ten years from now.

I started the process of thinking through my beliefs almost accidentally, when I was eleven years old, growing up in Switzerland. What touched it off was a squabble with my two sisters, Debby and Priscilla. We had nearly finished weeding the family vegetable garden, and we were hot, tired, and crabby. As I grew more and more obnoxious in my side of our argument, one of my sisters piped up and said that I wasn't being a very good Christian example to any villagers passing by.

Without thinking, I said the most shocking thing that came into my head—pretty shocking, at least, when your father is a minister. "Well, I'm not a Christian anyway!" I yelled. "I don't believe any of it!"

I was received with the dramatic reaction I'd wanted: shocked silence.

As we picked up our hoes and walked down the mountain path toward our home, I suddenly felt a tingle of fear creep up my spine. Inside, I had the dizzy sensation of standing on the edge of a dangerous cliff. I had said that I wasn't a Christian because I'd wanted to shock Debby and Priscilla. But now I wondered: Did I really believe in God? Was the Bible true? Did I have reasons to think so, or had I just blindly accepted what my parents had told me?

The more I thought about it, the worse I felt. I had loved this God of the Bible since I had been tiny. Now all that I'd

"Thinking is the hardest work there is, which is the probable reason why so few engage in it."

Henry Ford, 1929

heard about his teachings and his love seemed to be turning to ashes in my hand.

At the supper table, Priscilla announced, "Susan says she isn't a Christian."

By then I didn't feel like denying her words, even though I could see that my mother looked sad. I was sad, too, for I felt as if I had lost God and his love. I wasn't sure that there even *was* a God.

But I was also determined. I couldn't believe in fairy tales! I had to grow up.

That easily could have been my last day of knowing

How to Be Shallow: Key Words and Phrases

1. "Sorry, but I never discuss religion or politics while I'm eating."
2. "What did you do, swallow a dictionary or something?"
3. "I don't want to talk about it."
4. "What do you think this is, church or something?"
5. "Thinking gives me a headache."
6. "Do you like anchovies on your pizza?"

God was there, and that I was safe in the order he had provided. It could have been the death of my faith.

Or it could have been the end of my progress into thinking as an adult. All it would have taken was a comment like, "Of course you're a Christian, Susan," or, "You're only eleven; you don't know what you're saying," or, "Don't be foolish—it's obvious that the Bible is true."

But something else happened instead. That night when I was ready for bed, alone and quiet in my room, my father came in.

"Let's talk, Susan," he said seriously. "Tell me why you said you are no longer a Christian."

I confessed that I'd first said the words because I was mad. "But as soon as I said it, I was scared," I explained. "I can't call myself a Christian! All this time, I've only believed it because you and mother told me about it. Now I'll have to wait and see if it's true or not. Maybe the other religions are true. Or maybe there isn't even a God at all!"

There was a moment of silence. I still remember the quiet, friendly companionship in the atmosphere when my dad finally answered me. "Susan," he said, "those are good questions. I'm glad you've asked them."

What a relief! That dizzy, lonely feeling left me. It was OK to ask questions! It was important for me to find out for myself if what I'd believed was true.

As we talked that night, I discovered that my dad had asked these same questions about God in his own search for answers. Dad opened the door for me into a new adventure. He said that I didn't have to go through life with a blindfold on my mind to believe in God, merely clinging to hopes and feelings. Neither did I have to throw my beliefs out the window.

If something is true, he explained, you can look at it hard, and think about it, and compare it with other beliefs, and it will stand. It will be reliable.

I decided to do just that.

"No man can live without a world view; therefore, there is no man who is not a philosopher."

Francis Schaeffer, *He Is There and He Is Not Silent*

17

One way I've looked at all this since then is to realize that people are like plants. They need roots. A plant can appear to be growing and thriving. But if it doesn't have firm roots, it can easily dry out, be uprooted, or blow over.

Take a look at yourself. What are your roots? What is it that you hold onto to keep yourself going, day after day? Do you believe in things your parents told you? Television? Your school? Your friends?

Do you know what's really true?

And what will it take to get you to look for answers? You could wait, like Sally and Matthew, until you reach the end of your rope. But if you'd like to discuss it further, this book is for you.

"In ordinary times we get along surprisingly well, on the whole, without ever discovering what our faith really is. If, now and again, this remote and academic problem is so unmannerly as to thrust its way into our minds, there are plenty of things we can do to drive the intruder away. . . .

"But . . . to us in wartime, cut off from mental distractions by restrictions and blackouts, and cowering in a cellar with a gas mask under threat of imminent death, comes in the stronger fear and sits down beside us.

" 'What,' he demands rather disagreeably, 'do you make of all this? . . . What do you believe? Is your faith a comfort to you under the present circumstances?' "

Dorothy Sayers, *Christian Letters to a Post-Christian World*

A middle-aged couple stood chattering with me in a theater lobby. We all held steaming cups of coffee.

"How *purr*fectly lovely that you work with young people, Mrs. Macaulay," the plump Mrs. Briggs gushed. Her husband beamed. Then, still smiling, she launched into a major statement. "But surely you don't think that any one belief is right? Why, everybody knows that all roads lead to God in the end!"

"Yes, lots of people do feel that way. But are they right?" I asked. "If something is right, then some other things have to be wrong, don't they? If something is true, aren't other things false?"

The couple looked surprised. (You may have noticed that it isn't considered proper etiquette to express a definite point of view that opposes others.)

"Just think," I went on. "You have to drive home later on tonight. If I told you that it didn't matter which road you chose to drive on, it would put you in a mess. Why, if you were to get on the freeway here, you couldn't get off for another twenty miles!"

"Of course! That's obvious," Mr. Briggs sputtered. "We mean that you can't know what's true about something like religion."

The Briggses were mouthing a popular view, that there are some unseen things you just can't know the truth about. They think that the facts of religion are different from the facts of living in the real, everyday world of penicillin, grocery stores, satellites, pet dogs, and road maps. The truth in those areas seems quite clear. Obviously, if you didn't know the difference between *up* and *down*, you'd have a hard time getting to your class on the fourth floor!

If you sincerely thought that you were a cow, and

insisted that you should stay outside and eat the lawn, men in white coats would come and take you somewhere else!

But, religion, many people say, is different. In that area, any belief you hold is OK as long as you are sincere about it and it "helps" you. In fact, you can't say that someone else's view is either right or wrong, true or false.

You've probably already noticed this "anything goes" idea. Society puts up with a lot of strange beliefs and superstitions because of it: pyramid power, palm reading, good-luck charms, reincarnation. I can remember jumping over the seams in the sidewalk when I was about five years old, because I'd heard the saying, "Step on a crack, break your mother's back!"

Harmless? Silly? The little child Susan was playing a game. But there comes a moment when it isn't a game anymore. If you lived in tribal Africa and sincerely thought that you needed to eat a healthy baby's liver if the demons were to be appeased and you were to regain your health, would it matter? Could you be wrong?

Think of what happened in November 1978 when nine hundred people believed in their religious leader, Jim Jones. They were so committed to him and his teachings that, at his command, they drank poison. They gave it to their babies. These people were not simple savages. The poison was mixed by persons who had studied at some of the most advanced U.S. medical schools!

Every idea has consequences that grow out of it, as a plant grows from a seed. And the logical result of thinking that anything goes in religion is to think that any sincere religious action is OK. Even suicide or murder.

Though the examples I gave may seem extreme, they point out two things. First, what you believe about truth and right and wrong and God aren't ho-hum matters. Second, although many people might say that "anything goes" in religion, in actual situations they find themselves drawing a line and calling some religious beliefs wrong, hurtful, or stupid.

"It is important that a person choose the right answers in life," I told Mr. and Mrs. Briggs in the theater lobby that evening. "It is a personal disaster if he or she chooses the wrong ones. That is why I work in L'Abri Fellowship: we believe that there is *one* right road."

They shook their heads.

What you believe affects everything about your living every day. What you think and feel and do springs out of your beliefs. For instance, if you believe you are a cow, and then act like one, you might find yourself in a mental hospital one morning. Your beliefs might leave you in complete despair, like Sally in the last chapter, or with deep anger, like Matthew.

Later, when I was thinking over the conversation with Mr. and Mrs. Briggs, I thought that the following incident could have clarified what I wanted to say to them.

When our family first went to the old manor house in Greatham that is now L'Abri, we were given a huge pile of keys. We couldn't imagine that there could be so many doors to unlock—until we got to the property.

Our first task was to find the key for the main oak door at the front of the house. My five-year-old, Kirsty, tried helping me. "Is this the one?" she asked.

"Opinion is the queen of the world."

Blaise Pascal

"As one can ascend to the top of a house by means of a ladder or a bamboo or a staircase or a rope, so diverse are the ways and means to approach God, and every religion in the world shows one of those ways."

Ramakrishna Paramahamsa

Before I could reply, her older sister Margaret, aged eight, retorted, "No, that's too thin. How about this one, mommy?"

I looked at the key Margaret held up. "Well, yes, that looks like the right thickness. But it's the wrong shape," I said. I pounced on a more likely candidate. "This looks about right!" But when I tried it, it didn't go into the keyhole. It didn't fit.

I think that our search for the right key (which we finally found—one hour later) is much like the search for truth. The keyhole had a certain shape. Only one key would fit.

I believe that the world around us has a definite shape, too. All kinds of facts make up that shape. And I believe that only one explanation of truth and life—and only one religion or philosophy—will fit all the facts. The other options won't work. Finding the right one is like sorting through a pile of keys for the one that fits.

The basis of this book is the idea that you can find

Flying in the Dark

When I was a child in Switzerland, I used to lie awake and listen to the night. Where we lived in the Alps, there were no cars roaring by our door, and no voices or clatter from the neighborhood. We were quite isolated, so the silence was an interesting thing to me. I tried to catch the sounds of night creatures outside or the drip of icicles off the chalet roof.

Once in a while, the roar of a passing aircraft would drown the small sounds. I would feel my body tense up as I lay there, listening. How could a pilot find his way over the mountains in the dark? I imagined the drone of the plane's engine turning into an explosion as the aircraft plowed into a towering peak of the nearby Dents du Midi mountain range.

On foggy or stormy nights, my tension was even greater. Would the pilot make it?

the key to truth. But before you read on, you must decide if there's really something to look for. Do you think that there might be a key to reality? That some things are true and others false, some right and others wrong? I'm not rushing you into an answer; some people would answer yes to the above question, and others no.

What do you think?

I now understand how a pilot flies when he cannot see. He uses his instruments, of course, and he also uses a map. He has to have just the right map. If he climbed into the cockpit for the Alpine flight I heard at night and was handed a map of the ocean, he'd say, "That map doesn't accurately show the place I'm going to! It won't be of any help!"

Maps of the wrong mountain range wouldn't help him either. He had to have a map that described the area I lived in, near Lausanne in the Rhone River Valley.

We need maps, too, to find our way through our lives without crashing. We need a guide that shows us what life really is about. World religions and philosophies offer us many "maps." But which one fits where we're going? Which one will help us as we fly into the dark?

That is for you to find out.

"Some people say I'm a
Jesus freak,
And I do believe it's true.
Whose freak are you?"

Servant, "Holy Roller Blues"

I was cooking supper in the big, warm L'Abri kitchen. Outside, the cold winter night had descended, and through the window I saw nothing but blackness.

Suddenly I nearly jumped out of my skin. A strange and very white face was pressed up against the window! Even though I was frightened at first, I went to the door to let the person in.

When I brought the ghostly figure into the kitchen, I saw that I had nothing to be afraid of. My visitor was a thin, almost emaciated young man whose head was shaved completely bald. He was shivering with the cold and damp, and gratefully accepted a hot drink.

As we talked, I learned that his name was Joe, and that he was a young British student who had been searching for meaning in his life. He had met some members of an Eastern religious sect, and had been attracted to their otherworldly way of living. He thought these people had grasped the mysteries of the universe.

But by the time Joe came to us, he was so absorbed in this other world and so divorced from the real world around him that he was mentally and physically ill!

According to his new beliefs, Joe's own separate self didn't exist. He was one with all the other spirits in the universe, and a part of the one spirit: God. Spirit was all that existed. The physical world was only an illusion, he said.

However, as Joe lived at L'Abri, it became obvious that he couldn't function in the reality he claimed was the true one. He said he didn't believe in the physical world. But of course he had to eat—and he did.

He said he didn't believe in his own existence as an individual. Yet he would find himself saying, "*I* think . . ." Then he would realize what he was doing, and a puzzled look would

"I am plagued by doubts. What if everything is an illusion and nothing exists? In that case, I definitely overpaid for my carpet."

Woody Allen, *Without Feathers*

cross his face. Could he really say "I"?

In his search for truth, Joe had absorbed the idea that religious truth was beyond common sense, a completely different kind of reality. So he chose to believe what his Eastern friends told him, rather than trust his own life experiences.

A number of people and religious groups in the world would agree with Joe. They would say that you can't use your mind to find out what life is really all about. They may suggest drugs for finding this other reality, or meditation. This way, you can escape from your mind, and float into a kind of dream experience.

They make an interesting point that most of us don't think about: that we live by trusting our senses, whether we ought to or not. For example, if I were to ask you, " Does this book exist?" you'd say, "Of course! I'm holding it in my hand."

The Hindu and the Teakettle

One afternoon, my parents visited Cambridge University, and met with some students in the living room of a college apartment. My husband-to-be, Ranald, his good friend Tom, and other students gathered around the fireplace. A teakettle was whistling cheerfully on a gas burner nearby, promising hot cups of tea.

As the group discussed ideas, one young man from India, who was Hindu by religion, started to speak out against Christian ideas of truth. My father decided to probe this fellow's own conclusions, to show that he could not actually live and act upon what he said he believed.

"Are we agreed," my father asked, "that you believe there is only one reality, which includes all things, all ideas?"

The young man nodded.

"Then," my father pursued, "this means that, ultimately, everything is the same. Any difference we see is

But when you say that, you're making an assumption. You're trusting that what your common sense tells you is true. But how do you know you're not imagining what you see? How do you know that you're not imagining yourself?

The Chinese philosopher Lao-tse, who lived in the sixth century B.C., asked, "If, when I was asleep, I was a man dreaming I was a butterfly, how do I know when I am awake that I am not a butterfly dreaming I am a man?"

When I was a teenager in Switzerland, this kind of discussion about what existed and what didn't often took place in our living room. And it would always leave me hopping mad! I thought that it was some kind of stupid game.

I can remember shouting at a philosophy student once: "But *of course* the rose is on the table, and of course the legs hold the table up! This is crazy! Why, when my little brother was

temporary, an illusion. There is no such thing as a separate personality, correct? No final difference between good and evil, or between cruelty and noncruelty?"

The young man agreed again, but the others in the room were surprised at what the full extent of their friend's Hindu beliefs could be.

Tom was struck with the fact that such beliefs didn't fit into the real world. But instead of arguing, he reached for the steaming teakettle, lifted it off the gas burner, and held it over the startled Indian's head. Everyone looked surprised, and the Indian student looked scared to death.

"If what you believe is really true," Tom said firmly, "there is no ultimate difference between cruelty and noncruelty. So whether I choose to pour this boiling water over your head or not doesn't matter."

There was a moment of silence, and then the Indian rose and left the room without comment. He could not match what he believed with real life.

"The truth of Christianity is that it is true to what is there."

Francis Schaeffer, *He Is There and He Is Not Silent*

eight months old he knew that he couldn't crawl *through* a table leg! A baby is closer to the truth than you are!"

"Well, what *is* the point of all this?" you're probably asking, just as I was then. The point is a very practical one, believe it or not: you have a choice when you ask questions about religions and life views. You can assume that what you see around you and what you feel inside you are real, and investigate on that basis. Or you can assume that you need some special, mystical knowledge, and that thinking won't help you much at all.

People who hold the first point of view can look for truth by observing. People who hold the second point of view have to resort to more mystical techniques: blanking out all thoughts by repeating a single meaningless syllable called a "mantra," for instance. Taking drugs. Meditating on the thought of the sound of one hand clapping, as in Zen Buddhism. Or, just believing unbelievable things!

When I was a teenager, I was fortunate enough to be able to talk with people who held points of view different from those I'd grown up with. The Hindus voiced something like Joe's beliefs: everything around me, including the rocks on the mountainside, and good as well as evil, were a part of the eternal consciousness that was God. There wasn't a separate, distinct, solid *me*.

My natural instinct led me to disagree with these people. I felt sure that I had a personality. I didn't see how I could possibly live with thinking that I wasn't really me.

Joe lived in two worlds. His religion told him one thing. His senses told him something else. To stay alive, he had to do things his religion told him were nonessential or meaningless (like eat and stay warm).

But I believe real truth is practical and sensible. It fits in with—and explains—the world you see around you and feel inside. I propose that a good test for a view of life is to ask yourself: Can I live this way? Does it make sense with what I observe? (That question is one Joe should have asked.) A life view that is true would fit with the workings of the physical world and the facts of human personality.

If you don't feel that you need a practical sort of truth, then you can close your eyes, or meditate on your navel, and anything can be true in your head.

If you would rather use your common sense and your mind in your search for truth, you can continue reading, asking and looking with both eyes wide open.

"It seems to me quite disastrous that the idea should have got about that Christianity is an otherworldly, unreal, idealistic kind of religion. . . . On the contrary, it is fiercely and even harshly realistic."

Dorothy Sayers, *Christian Letters to a Post-Christian World*

Richard, a middle-aged man who somehow looked older than he really was, sat at the dining room table with his head in his hands.

"I've lost everything that meant anything to me in life," he sighed. "After my parents' marriage broke up when I was a teenager, I started drinking—too much. Still I managed to finish college, get a job, and marry someone who really cared for me. For a while I stayed off the bottle. Then troubles at work got me drinking more and more until finally, my own wife and children were frightened of me! My marriage broke up. I lost my job. And do you know what? Nobody cares!"

He looked up at me with a sudden spark of anger: "What a mess I'm in! If there is a good God, why does he let people like me have so much trouble? Come to think of it, why is there so much suffering in the world? It doesn't make sense to think there could be a God."

Richard's anguished conclusion was one I had heard before. Like many people, he wished that there was a God. But because of all the pain and suffering in the world, he didn't think a good God could possibly exist. He liked the idea of there being a God who planned things, who stood for right, and who would perform favors and miracles—something like Superman. But it seemed as foolish to hope for that as it would to believe in the tooth fairy. The evidence did not seem to point in the direction of there being a good power in control of things.

"Richard," I said, "I know you feel horribly trapped, let down, and miserable. But you must separate the two questions you're asking. First, is there a God? Second, if there is, then why is there suffering? If the God of the Bible is there, he is perfectly good and hates suffering even more than we do. The Bible says that although God is all-powerful, he also made the human race separate from himself. We aren't puppets! The choices we have made in history and are making right now have

resulted in an abnormal world. Much of what we see around us is the work of man, not of God."

Another L'Abri student, Allan, put down his fork and interrupted the discussion Richard and I were having. "Here you are, saying that the Bible explains how a good God could let evil come into the world by letting people have choices. But I want to know why you are so sure that there's a God at all. Isn't the belief in God the same as a gullible child's faith in Santa Claus, or the tooth fairy? Isn't it wishful thinking, because you want somebody to pull you out of trouble, and to tuck you into bed at night? Richard is right: the thought of an empty, uncaring universe is uncomfortable. But isn't honesty better than deception?"

Allan turned to Kit, a biologist from New Zealand, who had said he believed that the Christian answer made perfect sense. "I don't see how you have the nerve, as a biologist, to say you believe in God. You should know better as a scientist. What those religious guys experience is a blind leap of faith. Nothing more. Nothing less. There's no proof for God's existence! If I take off in a rocket for Mars, am I going to bump into angels on

Lost in the Forest

Imagine that you are hiking through a great forest, and lose your way. A storm sets in. You're relieved to see a hut in a clearing. A light shines from the window, and smoke curls from the chimney. You practically run to the door, hoping to find shelter there.

You knock. No answer.

You call. No voice replies.

You go to the window to look in. What a relief! The hut is occupied. There is a fire burning, and a kettle bubbling merrily over it. The table is set for supper, and a freshly baked pie sits in the center.

What do you know about this setting, using

the way? Or see a demon or two? Maybe I'll land in heaven itself!"

Allan had a valid point. In his observation of the world around him, he hadn't seen God. On top of this, he didn't feel he'd seen any proof of God's existence, either. He wanted scientific evidence.

Kit had something to say about proof. "Listen, Allan. As a biologist I operate on something that is the most obvious and reliable fact of all: the order in the nature of everything in the universe. Science operates on the fact that everything is orderly. Even though it is all amazingly complicated, certain causes always have the same effect. I can run an experiment again and again with a certain, sure result. Even the smallest child can quickly see that. You cannot even go home and make a cup of coffee without operating on the assumption that natural laws are orderly, not chaotic. You know that the stove's heat will always make the kettle boil; it won't freeze on the flame one day! So where did all this order come from?"

"It evolved," Allan said.

scientific observation? You know that someone lives in this hut, even though no one is home at the moment.

Someone had to have built the fire, put water in the kettle, set the table, and baked the pie. From the state of things, you gather that the person will come back soon to eat the supper he's prepared. You are not alone in the forest.

You cannot see the owner of the hut any more than you can see God or angels. Yet the evidence of that owner's existence seems overwhelming.

Try looking at the world as you did that imaginary hut in the forest. Do you see evidence of the hand of a Creator? Is the evidence as convincing as you would like it to be? Is there somebody at home in the universe?

> ## "Not only is there no God, but try getting a plumber on weekends."
>
> **Woody Allen,** *Getting Even*

My husband, Ranald, joined in. "The order we see in our world is the basic rule of all life. And yet, in mathematics, the odds of all of this order merely happening out of nothing, out of chaos, are virtually nil. To complicate the picture, we not only face the complexity of the mechanical universe, but there is also the nature of the human being. Here there is more than order. What about the facts of personality, love, kindness, cruelty, the existence of beauty?"

I had something to say here, too. "Allan, when I try to explain to children this idea that all things and people were made by chance, I tell them that my watch made itself. 'It took millions and millions of years,' I tell them, 'but the bits of gold somehow were thrown off of the planet in just the right shapes. Seventeen tiny jewels came together. I'm not sure just how, but finally this watch came out.'"

The students around the table laughed.

"Does it make better sense to believe that all the atoms, molecules, DNA codes, stars, and planets just happened?" I continued. "Children are often more down-to-earth than adults, for they accept that it makes sense that somebody powerful and intelligent created us. They can also see that this God could not be just a big machine or force. He had to think, to act, to feel. A machine could not produce the little boy who jumps into my arms, or the girl who composes sensitive music. An infinite computer could not produce the choice of love, could it?"

"I sympathize with you, Allan," Ranald said in the young man's defense. "In a sense we can't bump into God in the universe. But in another sense, I believe the fact of his existence bumps into us every day."

Allan had a lot to think about, but he decided not to commit himself just then. "Pass the cabbage, please . . ."

What would you have said if you had been eating lunch with us that day? Do you think there is a God?

You could decide that it makes sense to assume that

there is no God, that everything is the product of chance. Or you could think that it is more reasonable to accept the existence of a creator.

There is a third alternative. Some thinkers in history have come to the conclusion that there is no God, but have decided to pretend that there is, in order to give reason and purpose for living. "If God did not exist, it would be necessary to invent him," wrote the French playwright Voltaire in the nineteenth century.

But what kind of belief is that? It seems to be the worst kind of despair, to realize that what you want doesn't exist.

Actually, most people haven't thought through the three choices, but they live according to the third one. They say there is no God. But they act as if life does have a purpose from somewhere.

Allan had more than cabbage to think about, and so do you. Which view is right? Does one of these positions fit into the world you know, like a key into a lock?

Did the world come together by chance? Did the complicated human being, with all of his hopes, experiences, and choices "merely happen"?

Or could there be a Creator God? And if there is, what is he like? Where is he, and what is he doing?

"There is a hunger in the heart of man which none but God can satisfy, a vacuum which only God can fill."

John R. W. Stott, *Basic Christianity*

"The real security of being a Christian is knowing God is there . . . and always will be. Whatever problems and decisions you face, you're never really on your own."

Campus Life Magazine, "Welcome to the Family"

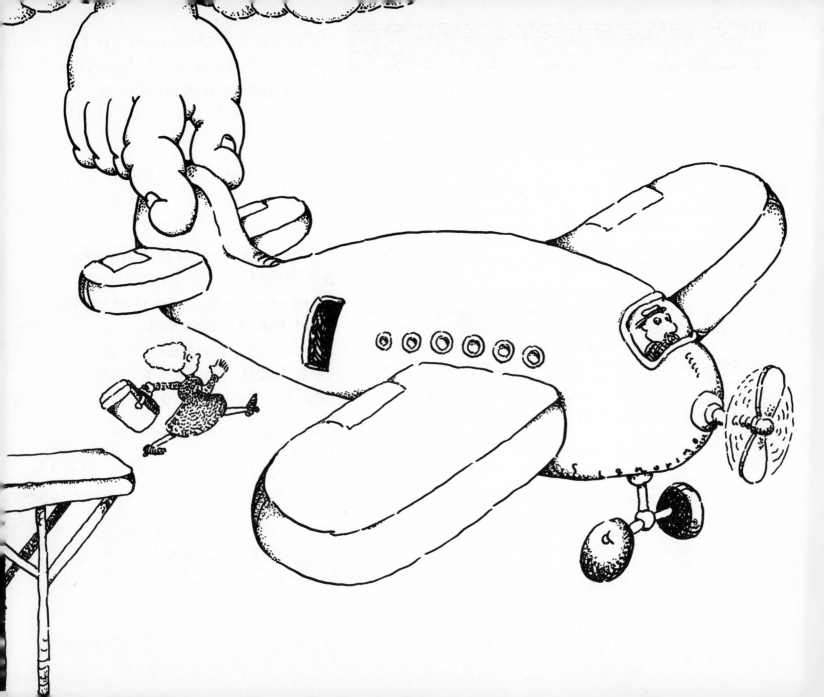

Sally, whom I introduced to you in chapter one with a bandage on her wrist, sat with me on the lawn one sunny morning. We had been chopping piles and piles of vegetables for a huge kettle of soup, to serve lunch to sixteen people at L'Abri. As we worked, we talked and watched a group of L'Abri students playing volleyball on the lawn.

I'd noticed that Sally's spirits had improved some during her stay with us. One thing that seemed especially to cheer her up was playing with the children.

"I've thought a lot about your belief that there has to be someone who made the universe," Sally said to me as we worked. "It makes sense to me, and it's very comforting—except that I don't know what this someone is like!"

She dug her bare toes into the grass. "I mean, I've seen some horror movies that really scared me! They gave me this creepy feeling that there were evil beings lurking in every dark corner. And I stayed away from dark corners for a while, believe me! You seem to think that your God is good. But how can you know that?"

What can you know about God? If you believe some divine being created the universe, you could conclude that this Creator is intelligent—more intelligent than we can imagine. Beyond that, you can guess a few more things about God.

You could guess, from looking at animals and plants, that God enjoys variety and beauty.

You could decide that God couldn't be just a supercomputer. How could a machine produce thinking human beings, who can love and can themselves create and appreciate beauty?

What more could you guess about God's nature? Could you say whether he is good or evil? You see both good and evil in God's creation, man.

39

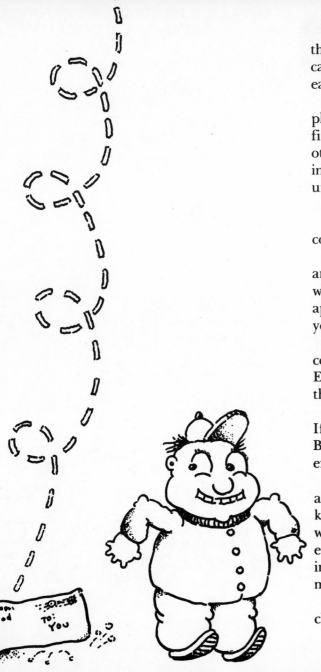

Could you say that he cares about the world, or else that he ignores it? If you look at nature, it sometimes seems caring, and other times looks like a cold system of kill or be killed, eat or be eaten.

"Well, Sally," I admitted, "if we called to the people playing volleyball over there and asked for ideas about God, we'd find the group agreeing on some things and disagreeing on others. And how could we know who was right? If God is invisible, and if he's so superior to us, how could we expect to understand him anyway?"

"I don't know," she puzzled.

"Of course, it would make all the difference if God communicated something to us," I added. Sally brightened a bit.

God communicating to us. What a wonderful, amazing idea! It's so amazing that we've almost all wished it would happen to us. At certain crucial times in life, you would appreciate hearing God's voice, or finding a letter from God in your mailbox, telling you what to do next.

"The Bible claims to be just that: a reliable communication from God to the human beings on Planet Earth!" I put into one sentence for Sally the most amazing claim there can be.

Is it possible that we do have a message from God? If a document claims this, we can test it, to see if it is truth or not. But what about a message from God through a vision, a voice, an experience? Can you test that?

Many people don't even consider the Bible's claim, and depend instead on their own experiences for their knowledge of God. They think that a miracle, or maybe a vision, would be more solid proof of God. Our culture is big on experiences these days, on finding things out by getting involved in them with your body and your emotions rather than your mind.

And there are some people you could meet who claim that they've had a personal experience with God or some supernatural being. Let me tell you about two totally different experiences two Americans had: Barbara and John.

Barbara had been searching for answers to her questions about life. She had enjoyed her European travel, but as she dropped into a lovely old English country church one day, she realized that these experiences hadn't helped her find any answers. Her prayer there echoed the cry of her heart: "If you are there, God, may I find you."

As Barbara left the church, her eyes caught a notice on the porch. She decided that the prayer meeting it announced in an English home would be much more interesting than an evening alone at the notel.

That night one of the women at the meeting gave her a book called *L'Abri*. It talked about the God of the Bible as if he was actually there! The book told the story of what had happened in ordinary life when a family had depended on him. It was amazing.

Back in London, Barbara rang up the L'Abri house. Dick Keyes invited her to come and discuss her questions. After spending a little time with him, she was armed with the new discovery that she could test God's communication to see if it was true.

As she boarded her plane for the United States the next day, Barbara wished she had heard about L'Abri before. *Then I could have gone on talking,* she thought, *and maybe I would have been able to find the answers.*

As the plane took off, Barbara struck up a conversation with the elderly man sitting next to her. To her amazement, he turned out to be a Christian minister! They talked all the way across the Atlantic Ocean to Chicago, and he answered more of her questions. The minister seemed to have been "placed" next to her just at the right time, just as the prayer meeting notice and the book had been. You could call that all coincidence. Or you could call it God in action—that's what Barbara thought.

"If only God would give me some clear sign! Like making a large deposit in my name at a Swiss bank."

Woody Allen, *Without Feathers*

Another person who thought God was speaking to him was a young Californian named John, who had an accident in his car and afterwards "heard" God telling him not to drive anymore. Over the next five months, the twenty-four-year-old John received more messages from God, telling him that he had a special mission to save the earth. At one point John unsuccessfully tried to gather twelve disciples to live with him in the woods near Santa Cruz, in union with nature.

John spoke frequently of a coming revolution, in which he was to play an important part. He finally left his wife and moved into the woods alone. A few weeks later he carried out his "divine mission." He stabbed and killed a prominent eye doctor and his wife, two sons, and secretary, deposited their bodies in the family swimming pool, and set the house on fire.

Think about both John's and Barbara's stories. They both thought God had communicated to them, but the messages were quite different! How could they know whether or

Wacky Facts and Fantastic Fakes—and What They Mean

Mrs. Mary Carpenter was on a boating holiday in East Anglia in the summer of 1938, when suddenly she burst into flames and was reduced to ashes in front of her husband and children. They were unharmed and so was the boat. There was no flame from which she could have caught fire.

The Ouija board at a séance in Flushing, Holland, some years ago spelled out the words of an English poem. Later it was learned that a young boy across the street had been learning the poem, concentrating on each phrase in turn, for his homework. . . .

Astronomer Patrick Moore sent a hoax letter to his local newspaper claiming to have sighted a spacecraft—and to his horror over twenty other readers wrote in confirming that they, too, had seen it!

Lobsang Rampa, who claimed to be a Tibetan

not the real God was speaking to them or guiding their lives? Could what happened have been chance? Or the work of some power other than God? You can see the problem.

Our culture encourages us to seek unusual experiences. We watch shows like "That's Incredible," fiddle with Ouija boards and séances, read stories about haunted houses, and admire people who have visions of God or who have supposedly died, seen heaven, and come back.

Yet an experience alone cannot tell you if the God—or force—behind it is good, or right, or true. Some people have amazing visions brought on by hysteria, dark nights, or an upset stomach. Others feel God's presence when they are singing a hymn with four thousand other people. Still others resort to prolonged fasting or to drug trips.

I think that this "experience syndrome" includes the person who glibly announces, "I experience Jesus Christ. He makes me feel good."

---

lama and wrote best-selling books of occult lore based on his biography, was revealed by a newspaper to be in actuality Cyril Hoskins, an ex-plumber from Weybridge.

Many people today are willing to build their deepest beliefs about life around supernatural phenomena they do not fully understand. . . . The proof of genuine spiritual life is not that we are able to perform one or two isolated, bizarre, and usually pointless supernatural stunts. It is that we have made the acquaintance of our Creator by believing in Jesus Christ, and can prove his existence daily in the new, purposeful, peaceful life he shapes for us.

We may not know all there is to know about the paranormal. But we can know God, who does. In the security of his friendship we find what years of supernatural experiences will never yield: the true meaning of life itself.

—**John Allan**, *Mysteries*

Well, that may be so, but drugs sometimes make people feel good, too! What more does this person know about Jesus besides this experience? And what will happen to this person's belief if his good feelings and experiences go away?

People who go looking for experiences will probably find them—but they may not find the kind they want. I believe there is an evil supernatural being as well as a good one.

That day at L'Abri I told Sally about Carey, a seventeen-year-old girl whose search for experiences led her into a trap. When in junior high school, Carey and her friends had started dabbling in the supernatural for excitement. They played a fortune-telling game. They went to a séance, and tried communicating with spirits. Soon, drugs entered. This seemed to send them into even more vivid thrills. But it all turned sour. Some of the girls got sick, and one died of a drug overdose. They were trapped and afraid.

My heart went out to Carey when she came to L'Abri. I wished I could turn the clock back for her, and undo the scarring to her personality! I wondered if she could find her way out of the occult. She was only seventeen, but the pull of evil on her was very great. I am sad to say she sank back into a foggy marsh of mental, personal, and spiritual slavery.

However, I am still praying for her.

"If only Carey had thought about who she was trying to communicate with, and why, before plunging in!" I said to Sally as I finished telling the story.

Sally picked up some carrots. "What is the difference between a frightening, bad experience and one that seems to come from God?"

"It is possible to sort out such experiences," I replied. "You can always test the message—the philosophy, the religion—and see if it makes sense according to the rest of what you know about God and the world. Does this experience seem to be the kind of thing God would cause, according to what you know about God? What you gather from the experience has to come from more than just the experience itself."

Don't get me wrong: I'm not saying that you can't experience God's direct work in your life. I believe that Barbara did. And I see God working in the world around me very often! Like the time my father, sister, and I were climbing in the mountains and got lost. We explored the cliffs, looking for paths. But when it grew dark a short while later, we knew we couldn't keep searching, because of the danger of falling.

So we stopped, and my father prayed. "Lord God," he said, "we know that you can see this mountain in the dark, and that you know all the paths on it. Please show us a way down, if it is your will."

Then my father began to walk again, leading us along. (We were exhausted, frightened, and not so sure we wanted to go anywhere!) We had hoped to find a path. Instead, after a few minutes we found a dry streambed. It led us down . . . down . . . down. . . .

I'll never forget the joy and relief I felt when we arrived in the valley. Although I could barely make out the shapes of cows in the grassy meadow, the sweet ring of their bells let me know all was well.

My experience led me to trust in God. It helped me to realize that I could pray about other things later on in my life. However, as I look back, the validity of my faith doesn't rest on that particular happening, however important it was to me then. The test came later on, when I tried out the reliability of this God and found that his truth made sense.

For me, seeing God in action goes right along with the certainty that he *has* spoken to us. Experiences are important—when they reinforce what he has revealed to us.

Think over your own life. Have you had any experiences that you felt showed you something about God or the supernatural? Has any of your friends had such an experience? If so, do you agree that you need knowledge in order to understand what such an experience means?

"Experience by itself proves nothing."

C. S. Lewis

"Miracles and truth are necessary, because it is necessary to convince the entire man, in body and soul."

Blaise Pascal

I was waiting in line in the Miami airport on a busy summer afternoon with a standby ticket to London in my hand. I had to get home to my family. There was nobody there to take care of the complicated needs of four children, a husband who at that moment was on a plane flying back to England after a conference in Australia, and the L'Abri household.

From behind his desk, the British Airways man looked down at me. "But, ma'am, no one with a standby ticket has gotten a flight from Miami to London in the last two weeks. We are fully booked for one month."

I had almost no cash, no credit card. I stood there, very alone and helpless. Deserted. I was in the United States because I had been caring for someone else. It had been the right thing to do, hadn't it?

"Please God, I have to get home!" I prayed.

The two crowded carriers' numbers flashed on the screen. The flights were boarding.

I went to another airline desk. Same story. Their plane was jammed, and they were sold out for weeks. The London flights had boarded; the numbers were blinking. All my hopes were fading, but I was still praying hard.

Suddenly an attendant came up to me and shouted, "Follow me!"

I ran through the airport after him, past an endless row of now-vacant lounges. It seemed miles, and the sprightly boy in front was fitter than I was!

Suddenly we were running down the gangway toward a plane. The gangway retracted two feet. The plane was moving! A stewardess held the plane door open, and I jumped the two-foot gap. The door slammed behind me. We were moving down the runway!

For a moment, I thought that I would have to sit on the floor right by the door! The plane looked full, and it nearly was. By the time I was shown to the one last empty seat, I did not have time to put on the seat belt before takeoff.

You learn in Sunday school that God parted the Red Sea. That was something. It's easy to believe in the take-home Sunday school paper! But what about in life today? The life of airports and overbooked planes? The airport attendants would have gaped with surprise if I had claimed that I had a direct communication system open to the Creator God. He had given me his open line, and a promise to help every day of my life. If I had put it to them that way, they might have even found a soothing psychiatric assistant to calm me down!

As the plane banked over Miami, my heart was still thudding, and I was panting and frankly incredulous. I did believe in answered prayer. But this? All the way across the Atlantic my heart sang, "O God, I can hardly believe this. Thank you."

I have saved that bright pink flight stub. Whenever I forget that the God of the Bible is for real, I just look at the family room door. *Oh, yes, the pink stub! Surely the God who can work in a crowded airport will not fail me now,* I say to myself.

By the way, this doesn't mean that every prayer's answer is "Yes." It is important to remember that the mighty God isn't like a machine that gives out bars of chocolate when a prayer is slotted in. There are "No" and "Wait" answers as well. Because God sees and knows everything, his answers are often different than we can picture as we ask.

The main point of such an experience is this: If the Bible is truth, then it is for life now. It is dependable. It has something to say about every part of our lives.

The two students had stopped their work in the garden, and were leaning on their rakes, arguing. As very little work was being done, I suggested that they come in for a break, and continue discussing with everyone. Soon there was a verbal fight going on!

"You can't expect me to think that something is always right or always wrong!" said Alison. "Sure, we have laws, but society makes them up as it sees best. The speed limit has gone from 70 miles per hour to 55 miles per hour in the United States, right? And abortion has also become acceptable, because we've seen that a woman has a right to do what she wants to with her own body."

Kit, the scientist, slammed his cup down, and countered, "But, Alison, you are only using words. You don't really live like that at all!"

"Oh, yes, I do," she answered. "You can't expect me to think that something is always right or wrong in any culture, at any time!"

Kit reminded Alison of something she had talked about at great length the day before. "If that is the way you really think, why did you say that one of our society's greatest evils is the way women have been treated? Now it happens that I agree with a lot of what you said. But I also believe that when you talk about something being fair or unfair, you demonstrate that you are a being who is moral. In other words, deep inside you know that some things are right and others wrong."

Alison was frowning.

Sally dove into the fray. "Well, it is pretty obvious that there is such a thing as right or good, as opposed to bad and evil. I remember how shocked I was when I heard that during World War II some Nazi soldiers had tossed Jewish infants into the air and practiced shooting at them as they fell. Who could

"If lovin' you is wrong, I don't wanna be right . . ."

"If Lovin' You Is Wrong," by Banks-Jackson-Hampton

disagree about the right and wrong of that?"

Jane nodded agreement. "Still, some things about right and wrong seem to have changed. Take the teaching of sexual morality. My school taught us that we could do whatever seemed sexually fulfilling at the time. They thought it was old-fashioned to say that certain things were wrong. In fact, you were looked down on if you wanted to save the sexual relationship for marriage. Even homosexuality was glamorous!"

All these students were dealing with different sides of the same issue: What's right and wrong? Is there a moral law out there that doesn't change? Or is morality something society can alter if it chooses? This is another clue to what the world and God are like.

If you had been in on this argument, what would you have said?

A common view today is that there really is no such thing as right and wrong. People often think of the universe as having no creator or purpose, and therefore no one to establish a moral standard or a way things "ought" to be. They say the practice of right and wrong is a matter of convenience, and that behavior codes can change from time to time. In such a way of thinking, there is no solid, permanent idea of morality, no such thing as a base for law.

Our afternoon's discussion went on to the ideas of the Marquis de Sade, a Frenchman who concluded two hundred years ago that this is a chance universe. It was then logical, he said, that there aren't any things we "ought" to do as human beings. The Marquis de Sade not only surprised people in the eighteenth century, but we find his ideas shocking today.

If he is right, then there are no rules. He said: "What is, is right." You can do what you want. What he sometimes wanted was to torture women for his own perverted sexual satisfaction. (That is why we use the word *sadism* to describe acts of cruelty done so that the person inflicting the "sadistic act" will feel satisfied.)

If the Marquis's idea is right, it is perfectly OK for a parent to cover a child's body with cigarette burns at will! The words *Be good* or *Be nice* would have no meaning. Instead you could say, "If it feels good, do it."

As we talked that day, the group concluded that very few human beings actually think this. We just know that some things are better, or *right,* while others are worse, or *wrong.*

Can you imagine a world in which right and wrong were turned upside down? British author C. S. Lewis suggests that you try: "Think what a totally different morality would mean. Think of a country where people were admired for running away in battle, or where a man felt proud of double-crossing all the people who had been kindest to him. You might just as well imagine a country where two and two made five."

Lewis did a survey of a number of the world's religious and legal documents, and found that most people—around the world and throughout history—agreed about certain ideas: respect for human life, care for family, honesty, respect for property, mercy for the less fortunate.

To say that there is no right and wrong seems as ridiculous as saying that pain doesn't matter. It reminds me of the young Indian student I told you about before, who said that he didn't believe there was any ultimate difference between cruelty and noncruelty. But his actions did not match his beliefs. He had to say: "No boiling water on my head. I can't live the way I say things are." Now Alison was another person whose ideas didn't fit the way she lived. She was saying that there was no such thing as right and wrong. Yet she was devoting her life to causes that not only assumed that there was a right and a wrong, but that those beliefs were worth fighting for.

If most people in the world do agree on a general standard of right and wrong, that's a remarkable thing. But where did this standard come from?

The fact that almost everyone agrees about these

laws makes it seem possible that morals came about just by people agreeing on them, as Alison suggested. She and other secular humanists like her believe God isn't there, and hasn't spoken. So we humans make our own laws. The majority rules and, presto! We have "right" and "wrong." If we change our minds about a law, that's fine, too. Or is it? Can we really act as if all choices between right and wrong are ones of convenience?

That afternoon's questions had been so wide-ranging that the discussion carried on the same evening around the fireplace.

Greg told us that he had been thinking about the issue as he was chopping wood for kindling that afternoon. "I guess a lot of us wish we had been stimulated to figure these questions out before we started living our lives any old way. It only takes a few years to make a big mess. I now see that if God has planned for us to live one way, and then we act in another way, we end up in trouble."

"There sure weren't any guidelines around for me!" Jane agreed.

Greg added, "The tv programs and movies, the words of the current songs don't help anybody. Television shows hint at premarital sex and sex outside marriage. All of my friends and I simply absorbed this view of how we should behave. We were being entertained, so we didn't question or think. We didn't answer back to what we saw openly in the movies. It wasn't pictured as wrong, and we never asked ourselves if we agreed or not."

Sally suddenly opened up with her own tale of personal sorrow. "Well, I made a mess living like that. In the end, I wanted to die. All the things I did just hurt me, step by step.

"I guess a lot of teenagers are like I was. I worried that I wasn't as perfect as I'd like to be: too many pimples, too fat. I wanted to be popular. I wanted to count as somebody important and have fun. Free sex was supposed to supply these benefits. It made me feel sophisticated and desirable to be

**"We have no secrets;
We tell each other
everything
About the lovers in our
past,
And why they didn't last
. . .
Sometimes I wish,
Often I wish I never knew
Some of those secrets of
yours."**

Carly Simon, "Secrets"

sought after sexually. I enjoyed the current songs, and they sort of reinforced my actions. What do you think happens if you take somebody like me, without any moral framework, and play songs like these for several hours per day? 'Got to have some hot stuff, baby, this evening. Need to have some hot stuff, baby, tonight.'

"But even though I had some sexual pleasure with some guys at first, soon I felt lonelier than ever. I felt used, not loved. Dumped, not cherished. Something had gone wrong! In order to drown my loneliness, I mixed in doses of alcohol and drugs.

"One day I woke up out of this senseless round to find out that I was pregnant! Old desires and dreams of mothering flooded back from my childhood, but they didn't fit with the new me. Everybody told me to ignore my fears, and so I had an abortion without further ado. Afterwards, I felt even lonelier than before."

Sally's eyes filled with tears. "I had dreams that I had left my baby in the attic under the eaves, and it was dying. I would wake up in a sweat with my heart thumping.

"When I saw other babies, I couldn't stop myself from thinking, 'My baby would have been that old now.' It was awful. I was in a black depression, and . . . well, you know the rest."

Sally finished her story with a strong conclusion: "If ever I have my own kids, I'll let them know that they *must* find out and follow what is actually right. I'll tell them what it's like to follow a wrong road."

Some people don't have a problem with the idea of man making up his own laws and then changing them. The question is, does this system of right and wrong work out in real life?

It didn't work for Sally. She had not thought sex outside marriage was wrong. Yet she found herself feeling lonely and used. She had not thought having an abortion was

"It is considered awkward to use seriously such words as good and evil. But if we are to be deprived of these concepts, what will be left? We will decline to the status of animals."

Aleksandr Solzhenitsyn

wrong, yet afterwards she was haunted by a guilt she never expected. Why did this happen?

One significant possibility is that Sally ran into trouble because she violated standards that were a permanent part of her as a human being. She had tried to ignore them, but she couldn't.

Let's examine more closely the question of where these moral "laws" we believe in come from. They aren't exactly like natural laws, or scientific laws. A natural law, such as the law of gravity, describes what happens on earth. If an apple breaks loose from its stem on the apple tree, it will always fall to the ground. It won't float in midair!

On the other hand, the moral laws we've been talking about don't describe what men always do. As a matter of fact, these laws are broken quite frequently—and each of us have broken moral rules we believe in. But we haven't thrown away the laws because of that.

Isn't it peculiar that we humans expect ourselves to do something that we have trouble doing?

The fact that the moral standard is difficult—and yet pretty universally accepted—shows me that it came from outside man, from a very powerful source.

"I'm not sure yet whether Christianity is true," said Fritz, a German student, after the discussion. "But it does answer the right-and-wrong question better than the belief in a chance universe does. The explanation in the Bible fits the facts we already sense: that some things are truly wrong, and that it's not just a matter of opinion. It says that, not only is there a Creator God, but that he is moral. He sets the rules according to his character. Even if everybody agrees to the same belief at the same time—such as the Nazi belief that Jews didn't have a right to life—that does not make it right. God determines what is right."

What Fritz said is one of the aspects of life that convinces me that the Christian answer is the correct one. What

Christianity holds true agrees with what I already know as a human being. That is, that although cultural standards differ somewhat, human beings all act as if morality is real and important. Right and wrong, kindness and cruelty, and good and evil are *not* illusions, because God is himself good, holy, and righteous. He made us able to choose what is right in what we do. And, because right and wrong are real, our choices matter.

Many people don't want permanent moral standards. They think man will know what's best for man, and they say, "Oh, but I think it is enough just to be nice and to try hard."

I'm glad they want to be nice. But what is nice? How do we know? And is there such a thing, anyway?

In the last chapter, Sally and I had been discussing how one finds out what God is like by looking at nature and at experiences. Another place to look is at human beings.

Look inside yourself. Do you feel some direction about right and wrong in your own mind? If so, where do you think it came from?

"There is nothing indulgent about the Moral Law. It is as hard as nails. It tells you to do the straight thing and it does not seem to care how painful, or dangerous, or difficult it is to do."

C. S. Lewis, *Mere Christianity*

When I was talking to Mr. and Mrs. Briggs in the movie theater lobby, they chided me for thinking I knew which ideas were true. "Why, young woman, you can't possibly know," Mr. Briggs said. Then he thought he'd make a joke. "Unless, of course, you've had a message from outer space or something!"

I smiled broadly. "Why, as a matter of fact, I have received a message—from outer space, you might say."

The couple glanced knowingly at each other. They were certain now that I wasn't just rude, I was loony.

I couldn't have been more serious.

When Sally and I had discussed her desire to know more about what God is like, we decided that we could not come up with definite knowledge about God all alone. Nor could we depend on what others thought. The natural world showed us some things about God. But it left us with questions, too.

"There is an ancient, reliable book that claims to be a revelation from the Creator of heaven and earth," I told Sally. "Is it true, or is it a fake? You have guessed that I am speaking of the Bible."

"But there are lots of other scriptures and philosophies, aren't there?" Sally asked.

"Actually," I answered, "as I grew up in L'Abri, lots of thinking persons came there who believed all sorts of things. I realized even as a teenager that there were not, in fact, many options to choose between!"

There aren't many basic "keys" of explanation of the world on the key ring. At the beginning of this book we looked at one, the idea that this is a chance universe. To me this is as absurd as saying that my seventeen-jewel watch made itself.

We also discussed the fact that everybody in the world knows that some things are right and others wrong, even though they may differ as to the details of what these are.

Therefore, I reject the key, or explanation, of the Eastern philosophies and religions. They say that ultimately there is no difference between cruelty and noncruelty, for instance.

There is another important reason that I can't even begin to consider that Eastern ideas could be true: common sense. According to those religions, there is no actual Susan Schaeffer Macaulay! And there is no you, reading what I typed one wintry morning in England! According to this belief, we only seem to be separate persons; we will eventually be reabsorbed into a kind of great fog of God. (That is why in yoga and Transcendental Meditation, people try to make their minds blank, try not to feel anything. It is because that philosophy says that, in the end, "I don't want to be 'I' anymore.") Personality with its choices and its appreciation and creation of beauty is actually a sort of dream. I fool myself when I think about anything, or when I love or care for anyone.

Does this answer fit into what I understand about myself and other human beings? Can I act as if that is true? No, I can't act as if I am a nothing.

Historically, there is a unique key, or possibility, that would explain the order of creation and also the existence of morality and personality. If the Bible is true, it would explain all the aspects of life we have been talking about, as I mentioned to Sally that day.

"The Bible?" Sally asked. "I've always thought that was only a collection of fairy tales."

Many people would agree with Sally. They might think the Bible is made of fairy tales just because it was read to them as children. They might think it's a bunch of myths because it talks about God and about miracles—and they don't believe in either one. But if they think it's merely fairy tales, they haven't really looked at it.

In answering Sally, I explained that the Bible claims to be something more than just stories. One of the Bible's authors recorded this outrageous idea: "The whole Bible [every

"It is my serious conclusion that we have here in the New Testament, words that bear the hallmark of reality and the ring of truth."

J. B. Phillips, New Testament translator

Scripture] was given to us by inspiration from God and is useful to teach us what is true and to make us realize what is wrong in our lives; it straightens us out and helps us do what is right" (2 Timothy 3:16, *The Living Bible*).

The Bible sets itself up as a pretty significant book! But does it stand up to this claim?

The Bible has been proven not to be a book of myths. It tells of God acting in actual history. Lots of people discard the "baby Moses story" and other Bible stories along with Santa Claus. But that means they never bothered to consider its claims seriously.

The Bible's text has increasingly been found to be historically reliable. In the last fifty years, archaeologists digging in the Middle East have again and again found that the text matches historical facts. The finds alone can't prove that *all* the Bible's claims are true. But it makes sense to assume that if the Bible *is* truth, it would be accurate historically. For instance, if the Bible mentions a nation, what archaeologists find should agree with what we read. And it does, so much so that the Reader's Digest book *Great People of the Bible and How They Lived* states: "By the end of the (nineteenth) century many people, including some prominent biblical scholars, felt that much of the history related in the Bible was probably myth.

"It was the discovery of the remains of the ancient civilizations mentioned in the Bible—the cities and monuments of the Babylonians, Egyptians, Assyrians, Persians, and Greeks—that eventually began to reverse the tide of skepticism. Throughout the nineteenth century, linguists in many countries worked to decipher the mysterious languages of these civilizations . . . and scholars began to piece together the history of the ancient Near East. It soon became apparent that many of the events mentioned in the Old Testament were, in fact, true."

In other words, in one sense, I need less faith today to believe the historical biblical account than people in my grandfather's time did. All the evidence found has pointed to the notion that the Bible *is* reliable. Many people have no idea that this is so.

For example, you've probably heard of the pool of Siloam in Jerusalem. It is a great tourist attraction today, for it is the pool where Jesus healed a blind man (John 9: 7). It is also the lower end of a long and remarkable tunnel, which the Bible says that King Hezekiah built to protect Jerusalem's water supply from enemy attack (2 Kings 20: 20).

In 1880 an Arab boy who was playing in the pool discovered an inscription in ancient Hebrew script describing how the tunnel had been made.

This inscription described some of the aspects of digging the tunnel, and confirmed the fact that it had been built around 700 B.C., when King Hezekiah reigned. It would take a whole book to describe these interesting finds that support the Bible's explanation of history.

As a writer, another aspect of the Bible amazes me. Consider this: dozens of people, from many different cultures

Cliff-hanger

If you were to visit L'Abri, you might hear an imaginary story that my father often includes in his teaching.

He asks you to suppose that you are lost in the Alps. Your view of the steep cliffs beneath you disappears into the fog. Night comes. Ice forms. It is death to carry on climbing.

You cling to the ledge with numbed fingers, and speak to your friend. "If we stay here, we will be dead by morning. I think we should jump into the darkness. Maybe there is a ledge below. If there is one, maybe we could have shelter until dawn. We will die anyway on this ledge."

That kind of jump would be a blind leap of faith.

But there is a second possibility. Imagine that you are on the same icy cliff. Fog swirls. Death approaches.

and separated by hundreds of years, all contributed their writings to a single work. The shepherd David hadn't the same education or social background as the apostle Paul, who lived in the Roman Empire. Job emerged from the mists of the very ancient world, while Moses was surrounded by a heathen Egyptian culture. These men were writing about the most complicated questions in the world. Some only told little bits of the whole, while others filled in the arguments in a later generation.

There were no telephone calls for consultation, such as, "Paul, what is your view on the infinite power of God, assuming that we enjoy free will?"

Is it possible that a tightly woven book would emerge from this process? That's what happened. The text is unified in thought and belief. The God it tells us about is unchanging. It is evidence to me that the Bible was indeed inspired, as it claims, by a single supernatural author: God himself. I couldn't explain it otherwise.

Suddenly, from away over the pass, a voice shouts out of the darkness: "I can see that you are stuck on the cliff. You can't see me, but I see just where you are. I am a Swiss guide, and I know that if you jump in a certain direction there is a safe, sheltered ledge below you. There you will be able to stay until morning, when I can come and get you."

Aha! This is a different situation. You can question the speaker. Is he reliable? Test his statements. Check out the facts. Then, finally, if you choose to, jump. It is still foggy, and you can't see if what the guide says is true. But it is not a blind leap of faith anymore.

In the same way, you don't have to blindly believe in the Bible. You can ask questions and test the answers. You can see if it fits reality. You can see if it's true, reliable, sure—and worth putting your trust in.

There is another feature found only in the Bible which provides further evidence that this book is what it claims to be: the Bible's prophecies.

When I was a child in America (I moved to Switzerland at the age of seven), I used to love to grab the newspaper to read the "funnies." I especially liked the Believe-It-or-Not section of the comics. How fun to read of a man who only lost his eyebrows when lightning struck!

To me, the prophecies (predictions) in the Bible have this same amazing quality. They came true, believe it or not!

For example, the prophet Ezekiel made a number of predictions in 590 B.C. about the destruction of the great city of Tyre. Ezekiel said that King Nebuchadnezzar would destroy the city, that the debris would be thrown into the water, that the city's site would become a bare rock that fishermen would spread their nets upon, and that Tyre would never be rebuilt (Ezekiel 26).

A ridiculous bunch of predictions? Not when Ezekiel was in communication with the God who shapes history.

Nebuchadnezzar destroyed the coastal city of Tyre in 573 B.C. after a thirteen-year siege. In the meantime, the majority of Tyre's inhabitants moved out to a nearby island and rebuilt Tyre there. Alexander the Great attacked the thriving island city in 333 B.C.—throwing the debris from the mainland city into the water to build a land bridge out to it. The island city was finally destroyed by Muslims in A.D. 1321, during the Crusades.

One modern historian has described the mainland site of Tyre as "bare as a rock," and has noted fishermen spreading nets there. The great city of Tyre has never been rebuilt, and exists only as a small fishing village named Tyre further down the coast.

Ezekiel couldn't have guessed that those things would happen. The story of Tyre and other similar ones help prove that God directed the writing of the Bible. All these

predictions couldn't come true again and again and again if they were just human guesses.

In addition to these prophecies, you can trace in the Bible the extraordinary, detailed foretellings of Christ's life, hundreds of years before his birth. One such incident may seem to be a "believe-it-or-not" fluke. But when prophecy after prophecy comes true, it is obvious that more than chance is involved.

Finally, and most importantly, the Bible shows me it is a true message from God because it answers the important questions of life in a way that makes sense. To me, it is like a key that fits. A girl I know named Ginny found this, too.

Ginny was the enthusiastic sort, and she was weary of the idea that life's aim was a fat bank account. However, when she turned to the thinkers of today, she was thrown into a depression. The more books she read, the more hopeless seemed the situation of the human race.

One day in Manchester, England, Ginny went into a bookstore and picked up *Escape from Reason* by my dad, Francis Schaeffer. She started reading the first chapter while standing inside the store. Slowly a joyous idea broke into her mind, like a sunny spell on a foggy day. *Maybe, just maybe this is true.* She bought the book, and read it on the bus.

Try to catch some of Ginny's excitement. She had suddenly seen that if the Bible were truth, it would explain the "why" questions she had about life.

You see, my father had come to believe that this biblical picture, or key, matches up to the way things are. It explains the order in the universe (creation by an infinite God). It explains our sense of morality (God is holy, and he created us as moral beings). It explains that a personal God created each of us as a separate person. (I am not a wind in a drawing, nor an absurd fluke of cruel chance. I am what I've known I was since the time I proudly rode my tricycle around the block at age three. I am Susan, a separate person.)

> **"God has communicated to man, the infinite to the finite. . . . The One who made man capable of language in the first place has communicated to man in language . . . about both spiritual reality and physical reality, about both the nature of God and the nature of man, about both events in past history and events in the future."**
>
> **Francis Schaeffer,** *Whatever Happened to the Human Race?*

Ginny bought some more of my dad's books, and was soon reading the Bible itself. It made sense! Why, yes! It answered the basic questions so well, it had to be the truth! Nothing else fit reality so beautifully.

After my explanations, Sally commented, "I certainly never knew that there were so many valid reasons for believing the Bible is reliable. It fits!"

Sally's interest and careful thought contrasted sharply with a common point of view put over another day by an American girl named Kathy, who told me, "I've always thought

How to Get Bored Reading the Bible

1. **Read it while the radio is playing, or your favorite tv show is on, or on a sunny afternoon when you wish you were playing Frisbee.**
2. **Use a version with large or old-fashioned words you don't understand.**
3. **Shut your eyes, let the Bible fall open and stick your finger on the page somewhere. This will be your "passage of the day."**
4. **Start reading. Read fast: Hethatsparednothisownsonbutdeliveredhimupforusallhow shallhenotwithhimalsofreelygiveusallthings?Romans8:32**
5. **Shut your Bible. You have now done your duty. You may return to whatever you wished you were doing in item 1.**

the Bible must be pretty boring."

Kathy had probably heard that the Bible was old-fashioned, or maybe that it was as hard to read as a philosophy textbook. But much of the Bible tells about real people: people who did brave or cowardly deeds, who were clever or stupid, who loved or hated. The parts that aren't stories have the human touch, too: poems with intense emotion, dreams, visions, letters written in love and anger. And then there are parts which claim to be directions for man, from God.

Boring? It can't possibly be if there is a God and he has sent a message to earth.

Old-fashioned? Well, people haven't changed much over the centuries, so the stories aren't outdated. If God is there, he hasn't changed either.

Difficult to understand? Once in a while. But if you have trouble understanding the Bible, try reading a translation that uses the same sort of language you use every day, such as the New International Version.

People like Mr. and Mrs. Briggs assume that the Bible is merely a collection of pleasant myths and religious sentiments. They do not realize that it represents one of the few chances the human race has for direction or for finding an answer.

If there is really a message from God to Planet Earth, telling us about our situation and what to do about it, can we afford not to read it? Isn't it worth considering—even if there is only one chance in a hundred that it is true?

These other religious scriptures all claim to give the truth about life. But, as you will see, they each have some problems.

1. *Stop the wheel: I want to get off!*

Some one thousand years before the time of Christ, the first of the many Hindu scriptures were compiled. Some of the titles may be familiar to you: the *Vedas*, the *Upanishads*, the *Bhagavad Gita*. The many Hindu scriptures often contradict one another, but to a Hindu that is not a great problem.

One teaching that most Hindus hold in common is that man is locked onto a wheel of birth and rebirth forever. But he can find release, either by following his life's path of duty, or by meditation. What is he released to? He thinks it will be a state in which he really doesn't exist, in which his soul is part of the universal soul that is everything. As you might imagine, the idea that one's self doesn't exist causes problems in practical living.

2. *Maybe I don't want off the wheel after all . . .*

Like Hinduism, Buddhism is broad and uses a number of scriptures, including *Tripitaka*, the words of Buddha, a mystic of the sixth century B.C. Buddha (Siddhartha Gautama) did not claim to be God, but merely a man enlightened about how to live. He, too, felt that life was a wheel, a birth-and-rebirth cycle of suffering, but believed that the suffering could be avoided by living in moderation in all things.

The Buddhist's goal is to achieve nirvana, a state in which he is no longer aware of suffering, desire, or his own finite self. If you think this sounds similar to Hinduism, you're right. And it has the same problems with practical life.

3. *How much do you weigh?*

   The *Koran,* Islam's holy book, was supposedly dictated to the prophet Mohammed by an angel in A.D. 610, and consists of hundreds of moral and theological teachings. Some Islamic scriptures contain codes of conduct so precise that the Muslim is told when to use a toothpick! But the Muslim cannot know if his life has satisfied his powerful and difficult-to-please god, Allah, until the judgment day, when his good deeds and bad deeds will be weighed on a scale. Although Mohammed claimed to revere the Old and New Testaments, his teachings often contradicted them. For instance, there is no Savior or Messiah in Islam. And women are considered almost less than human.

4. *You can't dig it.*

   The Book of Mormon, chief document of the Church of Jesus Christ of Latter-Day Saints, is one of the few religious scriptures in the world that claims to tell a history. It tells the story of a lost tribe of Israel that came to America before the time of Christ, and also offers some unusual teachings, such as the idea that God is an exalted man (Adam), and that men can become gods themselves through good works. But though Joseph Smith, founder of the Mormon Church in 1829, claims that *The Book of Mormon* was written by the lost tribe of Israel some five hundred years before Christ, the evidence shows otherwise. *The Book of Mormon* contains large sections taken from the King James Bible, which dates from A.D. 1611, some two thousand years after *The Book of Mormon* was supposedly written. And although the theory of the American Indians being descended from a lost tribe of Israel has no basis that any archaeologist has dug up, it does bear an amazing resemblance to the plot of a novel written in Smith's day.

5. *Don't take two aspirin: it's all in your head.*

   Mary Baker Eddy, who founded the Christian Science cult in 1875, built a religion around her book, *Science and Health, with a Key to the Scriptures.* The book includes many strange interpretations of the Bible as well as directions on healing ills. The principal teaching is that God is spirit, and did not create matter. Matter is evil. People only imagine sin, sickness, and death, and really aren't capable of them. So, according to Christian Scientists, you don't need doctors or medicines. You're only imagining your problems. Try to believe this if you have a broken arm!

6. *We'll just change a few words here and there . . .*

   Charles Taze Russell, who founded the Jehovah's Witnesses cult in 1884, wrote a seven-volume set of books called *Studies in the Scriptures.* Russell claimed his religion was the only true one based on the Bible, and that all the others in the world were wrong. Yet he used a deliberate mistranslation of the Bible, his *New World Translation,* to make some of his points. He went off track from the Bible's true wording most often in order to muddy the passages that indicate that Jesus Christ is God's Son and an equal member of the Trinity. This takes out the whole idea of God saving man through Christ.

7. *Would you buy a used car from this man?*
The Bible claims to be all the revelation we need from God, but Sun Myung Moon claims that we need more, and has written *Divine Principle* to fill the gap. Moon, who founded the Unification Church in 1954, claims that his task is to finish Jesus' work on earth. He says that Jesus did the best he could, but didn't accomplish his goal. So Moon had to come along and finish the job!
Yet Moon's personal conduct and many of the financial and ethical practices of the Unification Church are questionable.

It was Matthew's turn again to wash the dishes with Fritz, the German student. They were trying to think through a big problem: the evil in the world and its consequences.

I sighed. The bare winter trees made interesting shapes against the sky, and the day seemed to beckon to us. Nature looked calm compared to the questions now bubbling as hotly as the vegetable soup on the stove in front of me! Yet only if the answers to the questions were satisfactory would these two young men be able to go out and enjoy that windblown world of beauty.

I bent my mind to follow their conversation carefully. They had already mentioned typical examples of suffering and evil in our world. An insane ruler kills some persons in his own country, deeming them to be less valuable members of his "ideal" society. A baby suffers terrible injuries inflicted by its own distraught mother. A young father dies of a brain tumor, leaving a wife and child behind. Meanwhile, the leader of a vice ring, while ruining many victims' lives, sends his own children to a private school and builds an indoor swimming pool.

"Where is justice? Where is good?" Fritz stormed. "I believe I almost agree with the poet who said, 'If there is a God, he must be the devil.' "

Matthew and Fritz both disagreed with the Eastern view that God includes, and is himself, both good and evil. They admitted that the human being knows that there is such a thing as morality, and that this would be impossible unless God planted moral ideas in us.

Fritz turned to me. "Susan, do you think that you could explain what the Bible says about this? I never heard it from anyone who held it as a possible answer. Why is there evil? If this God is there, why doesn't he do something about it all?"

> "Imagine there's no heaven; it's easy if you try, No hell below us, above us only sky. Imagine all the people, livin' for today . . ."
>
> **John Lennon & Paul McCartney, "Imagine"**

71

"Well, Fritz," I said, reaching for a Bible as I talked, "if this book is true, the answer goes like this. The planet earth was planned and created by an all-powerful God. This God was not a machine, but a person who could think, act, feel. Though he is one God, he himself is made up of three persons: Father, Son, and Holy Spirit. So by his very nature, God relates to others.

"When God created, he decided to make more than just a programmed, mechanical universe. He created other beings who could think, act, and feel.

"As you know, the stars and planets keep to their courses, the swallows and geese migrate without fail, and apple seeds unfailingly produce new apple trees. These patterns are set. But in contrast, we are told that God chose to place into his ordered creation a new sort of being: a nonprogrammed individual. 'Let us make man in our image, in our likeness' (Genesis 1:26).

"This first man and woman on planet earth had a fantastic future. A whole perfect world to rule! And they could exercise all sorts of choices. They were free, not like the bird who had to conform to a prearranged pattern. 'Eve, shall I build a stone house, or a mud hut?' "

Knowing the sort of objections Matthew and Fritz were likely to be voicing as I talked, I added, "Now I know that you have always thought of Genesis, the book in the Bible that tells the answer to this question, as a fairy tale. But just for now, put aside your objections. Imagine: What if this was true? If this God is there, why not? He could certainly have started off the human race with one man and one woman."

Fritz nodded. It was obviously a possibility he could see. It was harder for Matthew to even consider. But he tried. Soon he became involved in the next part of the biblical history.

"So here is the situation: one man, one woman, free human beings. 'Free' does not mean that 'anything goes,' however. God is moral. The humans' freedom means that they may stick to—or not stick to—the right, by their own free choice.

They will also be able, because they are not some sort of robots, to experience—or else reject—love for each other, and love for God.

"However, this freedom carries an expensive price tag. The choices they make will affect their world. They won't be 'pretend' choices. They will be for real! Human beings have to take the consequences of their actions.

"Freedom and responsibility are features of real life we accept. For instance, one student works hard every night. At the end of the year, she passes her exam. Another bright student who didn't pass comes up and says, 'I wish I had brains like you.' This boy was just as bright as the girl. But he chose to watch tv every night, and in general never to study. When you choose wrong, you have to suffer the consequences!

"God gave these first humans, Adam and Eve, a test point to show their willingness to obey him. And he didn't leave them in the dark about the consequences. He spelled it out quite clearly. There was to be no stumbling into a mistake. In Genesis, chapter 2, we read, 'You are free to eat from any tree in the garden; but you must not eat from the tree of the knowledge of good and evil, for when you eat of it you will surely die.'

"Die? What a horrible word to bring into the bright, promising dawn of the human race!

"Meanwhile, another person entered the scene: an evil being who wanted to lure the first people to their downfall. Who was this creature? When twentieth-century man thinks that the universe is inhabited by other rational beings, this is a correct guess! The Bible tells us that before God created man, he created another kind of thinking life outside of our planet. These creatures, which the Bible calls angels, were actually higher forms of life than humans: more intelligent and more powerful.

"Like men, angels were also free to choose whether or not to serve and love their Maker. And one of the highest-ranked and most powerful angels decided to challenge God. He hoped to fight God and win, and rule the universe!

Many other angels joined his side. But the rebellious angel lost the battle, and was thrown out of heaven.

"The angel, Satan, who according to the Bible had originally been a beautiful and good being, became twisted and totally evil. The Bible refers to him with a number of strong, descriptive phrases, including 'murderer,' 'father of lies,' and 'ruler of darkness.'

"Right when Adam and Eve were presented with their test, Satan was slinking around the earth, scheming how to spoil the beautiful new world and the humans who walked it in harmony with God.

"Not to eat a certain kind of fruit sounds like an easy testing ground for the free choice human beings enjoyed. But when Satan, disguised as a snake, came to Eve, he got her to wonder why God had forbidden them to eat the fruit. Satan hinted that God was trying to keep something good away from Adam and Eve.

"Eve then had a choice. Should she trust that God knew what was best for her, or choose not to believe him? She

Someone Else's Spanking

I like to illustrate Jesus' great sacrifice with a story from my own childhood.

When I was four years old, my parents had a lovely antique table, on which the telephone rested. One day I threw a temper tantrum so violent that I tried to think of a desperate act to express my irritation. I took a wicked and forbidden object, a kitchen knife, and with fierce determination, hit this small table repeatedly, leaving deep gashes in the antique wood.

The inevitable result descended at suppertime. I guess my poor mama had been too rushed to see the table, but dad soon noticed.

"WHO DID THIS?" he boomed.

took some of the fruit, and gave some to her husband, who also chose to eat it.

"The Bible makes it quite clear that the decision they made was deliberate. There was a temptation, yes, but the responsibility for the choice had to be carried by this unhappy couple. They had chosen *not* to believe and obey what God had told them.

"The result: death. I personally have come to feel the horrible weight of this word on several occasions. In it are wrapped up all the other aspects of suffering: psychological and physical torment, cruelty, sickness, war, hate, hunger. Worst of all, there was the death of the happy relationship between the human being and the Creator. You see, God is good, love, light. And if these two chose death, that could not be included under the umbrella of God's fellowship.

"I sometimes wonder if the deepest pangs didn't hit Eve when, some time later, she gazed down at the body of her murdered son. This, then, was what God had warned them about. A human death! None of us can experience this for the

No use cowering. My guilt was established. Suddenly there was an unexpected turn of events. Eight-year-old Priscilla felt compassion for her now submissive small sister.

"Dad," Priscilla said, "I want to take Susan's spanking this time."

The whole family was thunderstruck by the offer. I was provided with a lifelong lesson when, after some anxious consultation, my parents reluctantly concluded that it was a fair offer.

I'll never forget the spanking my sister took for me. The knife gashes had been paid for by somebody else's love for me.

first time without being shaken to the core. But what about the death of a mother's own child? Especially when it is the first human death on the planet?

"So what have we now? God's independent creation said 'No.' The resulting evil was like the smell that occurs when a skunk is disturbed. The odor goes everywhere. In this case, the cancer of death crept slowly but surely into all aspects of life."

Fritz wanted to know, "Then, in the Christian view, is everything rotten?"

"No," I answered. "This creeping death still left some goodness, beauty, and love throughout the world. The good was certainly not all destroyed and lost.

"However, the human being faces a big, unsolvable dilemma. We were originally created to act with responsibility towards each other and our planet. A visitor from Mars today would only have to read one daily newspaper to see plenty of evidence that we have failed badly! But the ultimate consequence would not be reported in the newspaper. The biggest problem the human being faces is that we are now divided away from the eternal love and goodness of God. Yes, it matters now, just as it always has.

"Some people think of God as if he were a kindly Santa, sitting in the department store. A naughty child comes along with a confession. 'I bit my sister's nose.' The child stares up into the whiskered face anxiously.

"The bushy eyebrow gives the doting mother a wink. 'That's OK, honey, if you don't do that again, it doesn't matter.'

"Lots of people think that if there is a God, he must be like that kindly Santa. A little pat on the head, and there you are. But are you?"

There was silence as we three put away the last clean dish and took out a huge bowl of apples to peel for pies.

I asked Matthew and Fritz to think it out.

"There you *aren't*," I said finally. "The teaching about God in the Bible says that our choice does indeed matter. God couldn't sit there saying, 'Oh, yes, and here comes Hitler. There, there, I suspect your unhappy childhood left you with a power complex, and a chip on your shoulder.'

"This is where the reality of 'hell' comes in. If we say the human being is responsible for his choices, and if we admit the cancerous nature of evil, then we know we have landed ourselves outside the circle of light and truth and the comfort of God's love.

"This outside place, if the Bible is true, has a name. It is a place where we will go if left to ourselves. One name for this place is hell.

"If the Bible is true, a day will come when all men will have to face this Creator and be judged by their choices, according to what they knew. Even at the lowest levels of knowledge and standards, each one of us has failed.

"A lot of people are appalled at this part of the story, and at the many places where hell is mentioned in the Bible. They think it sounds cruel. 'Now, Susan,' they say, 'you don't really think God would send anyone to hell, do you? Or at least, he wouldn't send nice people, would he? He's far too loving for that!'

"But these people don't realize the seriousness of what Adam and Eve and all human beings after them have done. We are already outside the circle of life. A God of pure goodness cannot receive us this way."

Fritz interrupted. "That's a pretty gloomy view. Why, it's like a hopeless science fiction movie. The race is left to its own evil devices, spinning to its death in a dark galaxy."

"Yes, it is gloomy," I answered. "But the warm light of hope shines into the picture almost right away.

"This great, good, all-loving God responded immediately to the unleashing of death into the new planet. He promised that these human beings would have a new chance to

"I do not myself feel that any person who is really profoundly human can believe in everlasting punishment. . . . I must say that I think all this doctrine, that hellfire is a punishment for sin, is a doctrine of cruelty."

Bertrand Russell, "Why I Am Not a Christian"

77

have fellowship with him, because he was going to provide a way that the evil could be paid for by somebody else.

"You see, the idea was that God himself would come to earth and live and die, to provide a way for the price of the broken world to be paid—and for a new world to be started.

"So God's Son, Jesus, died in history. If you had been at the cross and rubbed the wood with your hand, you could have gotten a splinter in your finger. It really happened. Furthermore, Jesus rose from the dead, promising life forever to anyone who would believe. Yes, a real resurrection. If you had been there, you could have touched him, and seen his footsteps in the dust.

"It is this sacrifice of Jesus that makes Christianity such a different religion. Other religions list lots of acts or states of mind that have to be achieved before God will accept a person. But this message from God says: 'Yes, you are guilty. You have failed, sinned, ruined the perfect world. You can't be good enough. But I *love* you. I love you so much that my own Son came to your planet and shared your sorrows. He took your punishment.' "

I concluded my explanation to Fritz and Matthew with the most exciting part of the message from God. "If you accept this gift, you can come back into God's circle of light and love, and purpose. That choice matters, too. We aren't doomed to hopelessness."

By this time we had finished the apples. Matthew looked at me thoughtfully. "You really believe that, don't you?"

I nodded.

He went on. "If the Bible is right, would that mean that heaven is a real place, as well as hell?"

"Yes," I said. "The separation from God in hell is real. But if we choose to accept God's offer to come back into a relationship with him, Jesus promised that he was going to prepare a place for us: heaven."

While I started making piecrusts, Fritz and

"You're gonna have to serve somebody; Well, it may be the devil, Or it may be the Lord, But you're gonna have to serve somebody . . ."

Bob Dylan, *Slow Train Coming*

Matthew went on a stroll in the winter air to think and talk some more.

What do you think about the evil in the world, and how it came to be?

Do you think that a good God could be like a kindly Santa, and pat people on the head? Or does it make sense to you that there could be a heaven and a hell?

"Many people visualize a God who sits comfortably on a distant throne, remote, aloof, uninterested, and indifferent to the needs of mortals, until they can badger him into taking action on their behalf. . . .

The Bible reveals a God who, long before it even occurs to man to turn to him, while man is still lost in darkness and sunk in sin, rises from his throne, lays aside his glory, and stoops to seek until he finds him."

John R. W. Stott, *Basic Christianity*

One day, many miles from the L'Abri in Greatham, romance blossomed at the Sorbonne University in Paris. Philippe, a young and sophisticated French student, fell in love with pretty little Francoise, another student. The two began living together during the school year.

But after their studies ended, the lovers were not sure what to do next. They had to admit it was more convenient for them to separate than to stay together.

Philippe tried to shrug off his feelings for Francoise with some of the concepts he had learned in school. "Love is an illusion," he explained. "We only feel it right now because of the situation we happen to be in, and because of our hormones. But we shouldn't drag it on. Other people will come along to fill our needs." And so the two parted.

But Philippe and Francoise couldn't forget each other. They found, for instance, that the other sexual relationships they tried seemed empty. They led lives that they thought would give them fun and satisfaction—but found that the theory they believed in wasn't working for them. In the end, they came back together again.

"I don't understand why it is so hard to live without a permanent commitment," Philippe said to me later at L'Abri, where he had come to try to end his confusion. "It's as if we don't understand who we are."

We were sitting on the grass outside the manor house, watching a game called "Fox in the Morning," in which my husband, Ranald, as the "fox," was running after children of all sizes, who were the "geese." A couple of toddlers had to be avoided in the chase, and our dog Timmy complicated the picture with his excited barking at fox and geese alike!

Philippe broke into the cheerful noise of laughter and shouts. "You people are so lucky," he said, puffing on his

"Man is a machine in the sense that he is a complex system behaving in lawful ways, but the complexity is extraordinary."

B. F. Skinner, psychologist

pipe thoughtfully. "Everybody here at L'Abri seems to . . . Well, I know it sounds strange, but you seem to get a lot of joy simply out of living and being human. I've never seen anything like it before. I always imagined that Christians would be narrow, depressed, and boring people. Yet I come here and find that you throw yourselves into life. You seem to understand how to live it.

"I never realized before that the ideas I had about life were draining it of its joy. I have always believed that the human being was the result of chance. We're like machines, doing what we're programmed to do by our genes and instincts and hormones. So this means that I can't make choices: my genetic 'program' is running me. I cannot really love. A computer can't love! Beauty has no meaning. Relationships are a farce, an illusion!" Philippe ended his outburst and puffed on his pipe again.

Now, Philippe's view may seem to make life into a philosophy lesson. But, for him, thinking this way had meant that life didn't have much meaning or joy. "Francoise and I don't understand who we are," he had said to me. And that's it. If people don't understand who they are, their lives are going to end in personal and social disaster.

What are people? Well, there are two common answers to that question. One is that they are a high and complicated form of animal, operating from needs and instincts. Animals don't have any special value. The other is that the human is something more: an entirely different sort of being, able to create and choose and think and feel. Each one has value.

Have you heard of the book *Brave New World,* by Aldous Huxley? It's a fascinating novel written by a man who thought as Philippe and Francoise did. Huxley imagined what the future of our planet would be if man were understood as an animal, and controlled like an animal. All human beings were "grown" in glass bottles in a factory laboratory. There they could be conditioned before birth in various ways to fit in with a society that was all planned.

Never again would a person with a high I.Q. have to simmer with frustration at a factory bench. Instead, the oxygen was scientifically regulated so that a lower I.Q. was produced for a person whose life's function would be to put in four screws and tighten four bolts on an assembly line. How scientific!

Furthermore, a baby was conditioned to only want the "correct" behavior. Part of this behavior was random sexual play. You couldn't have two people falling in love! That would cause too many complications.

Yet, even though these unfortunate "persons" were genetically controlled and conditioned in every aspect, the fierce and independent human nature reared its head. Therefore, the population was constantly kept under control by a drug, a tranquilizing-and-cheering-up sort of potion called soma. *Brave New World* is a chilling look at what the world could become if man is treated as a machine.

The question raised by *Brave New World* and by Philippe's ideas is not whether such things as heredity, environment, instincts, rewards, and punishments have anything to do with a person's actions. Obviously we do have instincts, and we do get much of ourselves from our parents. The question is, do these factors have *everything* to do with a person? Or does a person have a choice in how he responds to influences around him? Is a human just an animal? Or is he something higher?

"Now, wait a minute," you may be saying. "I don't know anyone who really thinks he's a robot!"

You probably don't. Twentieth-century people often don't let themselves think out the consequences of what some scientists and philosophers say. They want to act as if they are special individuals, making real decisions.

But Kathy was one person who did feel the consequences of a low view of the human's value. Nobody at L'Abri that summer would have guessed that this girl, on a bike

"The universe was not pregnant with life, nor the biosphere with man. Our number came up in a Monte Carlo game. Is it any wonder if, like the person who has just made a million at the casino, we feel strange and a little unreal?"

Jacques Monod, molecular biologist, recipient of Nobel Prize for physiology and medicine in 1965

trip through Europe, had problems as serious as Sally's, for over Kathy's inner despair was a cloak of bouncy good humor. All we could see was an American student rollicking with infectious fun. The children were attracted to her like bees to a honeypot.

But late one night, Kathy shed her outward appearances. I was sorting laundry, and she came into the laundry room. Soon our quiet surroundings led to a friendly sharing of the children's antics. She told me how much fun she had with my little four-year-old daughter, Fiona. This led to a sad description of Kathy's own insecure childhood.

"It really shattered my life when my parents' marriage broke up," she began. "I was thirteen, and I couldn't get it out of my head that somehow *I* was responsible for the breakup. Everybody had been so grouchy and disapproving of me for so long, that I figured it all must be my fault.

"I never felt accepted or at home anywhere again. Things went from bad to worse. Both of my parents not only

84

married again, but divorced again. Even my grandparents decided to be 'honest,' and their marriage split up. I felt like a refugee!

"As I went through school, I was very mixed up. I felt unsure of myself, so I tried to do anything that I thought would get other kids to accept me. If they were smoking, I'd smoke. If a boy wanted something sexual from me, I'd give in. When drugs were passed out, I'd try them. All the time I was really crying, 'Am I worth anything to anybody?'

"I tried to look beautiful. I tried to be popular. I tried for top grades, and dreamed of a high-status career. But by the time I got to college, I'd decided that I was a nobody, and life was a big hoax. Everybody was just going through the motions of living, pretending that what they thought and chose really mattered. You could only exist if you put on an act to other people as well as to yourself. Well, my act broke down. I couldn't handle it anymore. The college sent me to a psychiatrist."

Mind
Standard preprogrammed computer with 64K memory. Additional memory available, plus programs for advanced math, creativity, love, politics, etc. (Ask your dealer about software.)

Face
Male: Erik Estrada. Female: Brooke Shields. Choose white, black, brown, red, or yellow. Custom face stylings available at additional cost.

Individual Will/Soul
Not available. Ask your dealer about simulated will/soul programming and software for *Mind*.

See your local people dealer today! Offer good while supply lasts.

"If . . . ever . . . man was only an animal, we can if we choose make a fancy picture of his career transferred to some other animal . . . in which elephants built in elephantine architecture . . . in which a cow had put on four boots. . . .

Man has distanced everything else with a distance like that of astronomical spaces. . . . It is when we regard man as animal that we know he is not."

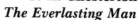

G. K. Chesterton
The Everlasting Man

Although Kathy had been made insecure by her family's breakup, this wasn't the only reason she felt that she had no worth. She wanted to matter as a person, but she had no basic reason for believing that she did. She was just another human animal on the planet for a few years.

If you, like Kathy, feel something inside that rebels against the idea of not having any lasting value, or if you wish, like Philippe, that you had real freedom and choices, you do have another option. You can decide that you must have something called a *will*, and an individual personality that is more than the sum of all those biological influences.

But if we do have will, choice, and freedom, where did these things come from? Scientists don't see anything comparable to personality traits in animals; they act in order to meet their simple needs for food and shelter and survival —nothing more. And if chance brought us up from animals, we're nothing more than sophisticated versions of them.

But the Bible has an explanation of where man's personality comes from. On the very first page of the Bible, the writer of Genesis explains that God created the human being in his own "image." The human, according to the Bible, is thus different from the other creatures God made. Created "in God's image" means created with some of the characteristics that God has: the ability to think, to love and feel emotions, to choose.

As you read in the last chapter, God offered the first man and woman choices—and held them responsible for what they did.

Thus, man's personality didn't evolve up from animal life, according to the Bible. It was handed down from a higher source: God. This gives man a free will. It also makes him a special creature with value.

For me, the Bible's teaching here fits the keyhole of reality, and what I observe as the truth about the way people are. After all, if I know much about anything, I know about myself! I know that I've made real choices: some good and some terrible.

I've loved and, unfortunately, I've hated. There may be many strong influences on me, but the person I am is more than just responses to those influences. I am somebody. I have value. I don't have to just go through the motions. And that is what Kathy realized at L'Abri.

"You'll never know what coming here did for me," she said. "I was jolted out of my nightmare by the simplicity of the situation: hearing you chat about how to make soup out of spinach leaves, listening to the Narnia stories read out loud after Sunday tea, having Fiona snuggle up on my lap. It all started making sense. Human life really matters! I feel like a frozen statue that is thawing out. I want to be a Christian, too."

I asked Kathy a few questions to make sure she understood and believed in the Bible's explanation of life. Yes, she believed that God existed. Yes, she knew she was a sinner; her choices, even her bad ones, had not been make-believe, but had mattered. Yet, even though she had chosen the wrong, she believed God had sent his Son to provide the way back into his kingdom—because he cared for her.

One last step remained for Kathy. She bowed her head and said, "Thank you, God. I accept your gift for me."

Kathy found a new self-knowledge and understanding of her personal worth after she decided that the Bible was truth, and she chose to accept its offer. Her "act" was over.

She discovered that she could now relax and look around as an accepted and loved human being. God had said, "You matter. You are so precious that I would have come to your planet if you were the only human being who would accept my offer."

That put her on a new footing. Slowly, the reality of what this meant sank in. For instance, she knew God had made nature for her to enjoy. As Kathy went on long Sunday afternoon walks over hills and through woods, she reveled in their beauty. In fact, she was inspired to begin painting again,

something that she had stopped long before. She said to me, "I feel free to live."

Do you get a glimmer of how exciting all of this is? If Christianity is true, then we have the basis for appreciating first ourselves and then other people. We can see how worthwhile it is to fulfill our potential. For one person, this may mean writing plays or directing films. Someone else draws and paints. Everything we do can have value: cooking a meal for a family group to enjoy, or making a beautiful garden out of a grubby backyard. Relationships matter, just as Philippe and Francoise found. So it is not a "waste of time" for me to sit on a front porch visiting my grandparents.

Human ideas have meaning and interest. Some are right, others wrong. Some helpful, others destructive. Therefore, I shouldn't act as if my head were a block of cement and give it a continuous junk diet of soap operas, cheap fiction, and bad music.

All in all, I can be glad to be a human being!

Unfortunately, some Christians don't see the implications of what they believe. This leads to the strangled sort of human life Philippe expected of Christians. These people make the mistake of thinking that ordinary life isn't as important as "spiritual" activities, such as attending prayer meetings and reading Christian books. They think that to be Christian, they have to "be spiritual" every minute.

Now, I'm not saying that you should neglect the directly "spiritual" aspect of life. If God is there, it is a relief to be able to talk to the one who loves and knows us completely! Furthermore, the Bible is a lifelong lifeline to grow in the understanding of God's truth. The more we search the Bible, the more we will grow and understand. We also need to discuss and pray with other Christians.

But it is also an important part of life to enjoy a sunset on a beach. Understanding who I am means that I can throw myself into the fullness of life. I can come out of the waves to relish in a picnic supper, cooked over a beach bonfire. I don't have to feel I'm wasting time when I pour hours into learning to play the piano or into writing songs. If I marry, this means enjoying the physical, sexual side of that experience. I delight in as full a life as possible. The life of a human created by God is full of exciting facets.

Philippe knew how different these ideas made the living of life.

Kathy experienced a profound change.

What do you think about yourself? Do you feel the influence of things like heredity on your actions? The influences of your environment: pleasure and pain and so on?

If so, do you believe that there is something else unique inside you and all other people that cannot be explained by the idea that you are a machine or animal? Do your ideas of love and beauty and your choices mean anything, or are they all illusions?

Do you have value?

"The Bible tells us who we are. . . . We do not need to be confused, as is much of modern mankind, about people's distinction from both animal life and . . . complicated machines. . . . Suddenly people have unique value."

Francis Schaeffer, *Whatever Happened to the Human Race?*

Chapter Ten

"Defective merchandise: please discard."

The birth of Liz's third baby had been quick. She heard a hearty cry, and a sense of excited happiness swept over her.

"It's a boy!" the doctor said.

Her husband, Tim, gave her a sip of water, and they waited for the baby to be handed to them. There was a strange delay.

Liz caught the doctor's eye. "Is my little boy OK?"

The doctor was busy. He didn't answer right away. He was wishing for the good old days, when that bright-eyed young mother would have been unconscious, and the father safely out in the hall. He carefully covered up the baby's spine with a dressing. It was open to infection, because it hadn't closed over normally. Then he was able to wrap the baby up and give it to Liz to hold in her arms.

The sweet little head dispelled Liz's first fears. The doctor had acted oddly, but things couldn't be too bad! Two bright black eyes blinked up at her. She stroked the hair, touched the ears. Her baby! Her first boy!

The next morning, a specialist came to talk to the parents about their little baby. At first Liz and Tim were stunned by what they were told, then angry, then grieved. The doctor tried to be kind, but the truth wasn't. "His spinal cord never closed up properly before he was born. This means that he needs an operation to cover over his spine and also to drain fluid from his brain. With this treatment he'd live, but be handicapped—I can't say how badly at this stage. Many children like him never walk normally, and are not able to control their bladders."

Tim broke in. "When can you operate?"

The doctor cleared his throat and went on to say that handicapped children were such an extra stress factor in a family that their parents' marriages often broke up. His suggestion was that it would be better not to operate. Sooner or later the baby would die, drugged and unaware of the life that he was to miss.

Do you think that I am making this story up? I wish I was. But similar decisions are now being made every day. These young parents had encountered a medical doctor who believed what Philippe had been taught: that man is merely a higher sort of animal.

This doctor's beliefs had consequences in his actions. Animals and machines are objects we find useful, right? When they are no longer useful, or when something goes wrong with them, we discard them. The doctor saw Tim's and Liz's baby as being much like a piece of defective equipment. In his opinion, the child would never be physically perfect, had too many limitations to live with, and would cause his parents too much extra work.

Tim had an almost uncontrollable urge to get up and punch the doctor hard in the nose. "You don't seem to understand that this isn't a manufactured product that has gone wrong! My little son isn't of less value as a person than those of us with two good legs! As Christians, we believe that each human being has unique value in God's eyes. We all have something more or less wrong to cope with in life. If I hadn't heard you with my own ears, I wouldn't have believed that any doctor could say what you just said! This is our child!"

If the human being is merely a complicated machine, dropped by chance into the universe, then it is nonsense to fight for the rights of any one particular individual. So, for example, many women have been hoodwinked into abortions, into believing that the tiny, separate human being that grows within their wombs is a sort of tumor. They hear words and phrases such as: "Inconvenient." "Unwanted." "Imperfect." "Will ruin your life-style." "Just a blob of tissue."

However, when a similar "blob" happens to be a planned baby, these women croon over the miracle of a new, separate life. The brain and the heart of the unborn child is functioning by the time the woman realizes she is pregnant. The expectant mother may say things like: "What a lively baby. I think it's going to be in the Olympics!"

How far away are we from the society of *Brave New World* when we choose who will be allowed to live? Are only the planned-for, the perfect, and the healthy given a right to life?

This has been the logical outcome of the man-as-animal thinking today: we allow people to kill off their unwanted babies.

The next logical step is horrible. If it is OK to destroy human life before birth, then it is equally all right to let newly born life die if it is defective. I read about a tribe of Africans who thought that twins were abnormal. One hapless babe would have its mouth packed with ashes, and be left out under a thornbush.

Another tribe said that a handicapped child was a "monkey." Since monkeys belong in trees, the handicapped newborn was placed there to die.

In many heathen cultures, any female was viewed as a lower and often unwanted creature. Little girls were once left to die in China.

We renounce such practices as primitive. Yet Tim and Liz ran into similar discrimination against a handicapped child in a civilized country today.

And, strangely enough, there have started to be abortions performed in the United States when tests show that the baby is not the sex desired by the parents. I found it a curious sociological throw-back when I read that so far most of these abortions have been to get rid of an unwanted *female* child!

But what could make people always valuable? Though many Westerners behave as if they believe humans are special, they do not know why this should be so.

Here God's message, the Bible, steps in and offers an explanation. People are something special because God made them *in his own image*. This obviously doesn't mean we look like

"Father of the Year? Nobel physicist and genetic theorist William Shockley told an interviewer that his own three children 'represent a very significant regression' and attributed their shortcomings to their mother, who 'had not as high an academic achievement standing as I.'"

"Dubious Achievement Awards," *Esquire*, **January 1981**

God—because he is a spirit. Nor do we have his infinite power and knowledge. But we do have personality as he does, and the ability to think, have emotions like love, and make choices within our limitations. We are a mixture, a personality which is "like God's" in a physical body that is part of the earth God created.

Each human being has one hundred percent value in God's sight, regardless of age, sex, I.Q., physical fitness level, race, or psychological condition. In fact, God's Son on earth, the Lord Jesus, showed particular respect to the people society

Jos

Little Jos looked ahead with a blank face. His nose was running, and he never moved in his stroller. He had been "mentally defective" since birth. Most people tended to leave him alone. His mother had agonized fears about him.

She certainly had her hands full. She had lively twins of four years: a blonde girl and a dark, lively boy. Now she was trying to cope with the guilt and fear of this seemingly useless eighteen-month-old baby.

When Jos was lifted out of the stroller, he would smile and respond. But most of the time he seemed in a fog, content just to sit.

His mother was a frequent visitor at our house, and she let Jos play with the other toddlers. He seemed to be "reached" through music, and would clap and laugh when we played a record.

I had a strong intuition about Jos. "I don't care what anybody claims," I told the mother. "There is no such thing as a human vegetable. There is a lovely little person called Jos in there, and the physical mechanism has been somehow damaged. But his personality isn't. We must struggle to make contact with him."

Jos was soon coming to Sunday school. He loved clapping to the singing, and his eye seemed to catch mine more abhorred: the prostitute, the leper, the hated Samaritan, the woman. Religious Jewish leaders used to pray every day, "Thank God I was not born a woman." But the woman, the handicapped person, and the outcast always found that Jesus respected them as individuals.

And so, the true Christian world view has always led to a respectful kind of behavior towards fellow human beings. We must beware of the mind-numbing influence of ideas around us! We can be hoodwinked if we listen to what

---

and more often. He soon was reaching out for his brother's and sister's toys at home. Little Jos was communicating in pleased grunts within the year. Somehow, I think that his struggle to understand and operate in our world made him into an especially lovable little boy.

Jos is fourteen now. He has made tremendous progress both at home and at school. I wonder what the doctor would say if he could see this fine boy today? He had predicted that Jos was going to be "like a vegetable" all his life.

If I ever meet that doctor, I will say: "Come with me, sir. You've done so well that you now enjoy a home in the choicest area of town. But come see Jos. He, too, is a unique human being. His struggle has been as valiant as yours, even though a solo shopping expedition is a major triumph for him. He is a young person who is in communication with the Creator of heaven and earth. He prays. And, yes, he can even read simple Scripture passages. He swims and enjoys playing a rather lopsided game of soccer! He is actually more help at home than any of the other children. He cheerfully clears the table, cleans the rooms, and is generally his mother's right-hand man. He is loved and respected.

"Who could dare to say that Jos as a person is of less value than someone with a higher I.Q. score?"

Remember Jos.

> **"People are special and human life is sacred, whether or not we admit it. . . . Every person is worth fighting for, regardless of whether he is young or old, sick or well, child or adult, born or unborn, or brown, red, yellow, black or white."**
>
> **Francis Schaeffer, *Whatever Happened to the Human Race?***

"everybody" is thinking. It was a mind-boggling deception when the Supreme Court of the United States stated in 1857 that a black person could not become a citizen. They now, thankfully, have revoked that. But what about the unborn child? Did you know that, according to the same court, he or she is now considered nonhuman, and enjoys no legal protection? If we don't take care, the next step on this slippery slope will be that the handicapped are "nonpersons." Others will slowly fall into this category, as our minds are dulled.

I'd like to think back to the novel, *Brave New World*. Each "person" was only a cog in the machine of society. He could not choose, love, think, or be creative. He couldn't alter his preprogrammed path. When these people reached the accepted end of their biological life span, they were carted off to a special place. There, with any remaining brain dimmed by the drug soma, the elderly person stared at a tv set, which lulled him into a stupor as he died. Soon the ashes of his cremated body dispersed into the sky.

How do we view the old person today? Are we far from *Brave New World*?

Our society has certainly stopped thinking of elderly people as useful. They have to retire at a certain age, and after that are often dumped into nursing homes or rest homes by uncaring relatives or by the state. The elderly are castoffs—not killed, necessarily, but certainly neglected.

And sometimes the question of life and death does come in. Should an eighty-year-old with some terminal disease be treated? Isn't his life all but over anyway? The questions get complicated. Some people feel an elderly person's life can be ended by "euthanasia," or "mercy killing."

The Christian view of man, based on the Bible, says that our value is not determined by our age or how much money we make, or how "useful" we are any longer. Therefore, we are to treat the aged with dignity, care, and respect. It *is* a damaged world we live in, and that is why eyesight fails, knees get stiff, and the body "machine" winds down. We are all caught up in this process, and a person is not less human when he is more in time's grip.

When I see a neglected huddle of old people today, I remember the sturdy old Swiss ladies who farmed and lived in the Alpine valley where I grew up. I have a hard time relegating someone into the "worn-out" category when I remember these women! They continued making hay under the hot summer sun, evidently unaware that they could possibly be past such labor! The work consisted of raking up every last stalk of precious grass—from nearly vertical hillsides! The women's long black skirts looked hot, but they managed to work in them from dawn to dusk.

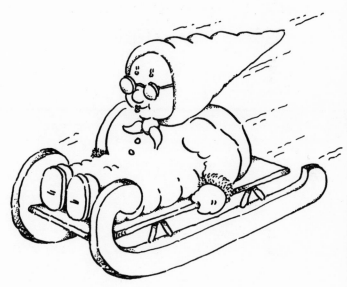

Even in winter, there was no mindless rest for these ladies. How I loved to see them sledding on the clean, snowy roads! Some lived in tiny chalets several miles from the village. The transport down the mountain was free. The old woman would seat herself on the sled, sit ramrod straight, lift her feet, and shoot down with frightening speed. The sled was guided around hairpin bends by the single touch of a heel!

I would often visit these old women. They were my best friends. Their faces were wrinkled by a hard life, and they delighted in telling me tales of their pasts. I am glad that I knew them while I was young. Their activity in old age reassures me that I can keep on being fit! Also, their unique personalities have spiced my whole experience of life.

What happens when a society puts a low price tag on the value of some kinds of human life? All human life is then less special. There is no longer any reason to listen to the ancient law, "Thou shalt not kill." People can begin to say, "This stage of life can be skipped," or, "This condition of life is too hard to care for," or, "This life is not worthy to be lived."

Fortunately, many people do hold the Christian views that any human life is valuable. You'll be glad to hear that Tim and Liz found another doctor who was skilled and ready to help their little boy, Paul. The extra effort Paul has put into getting through his first years gives him a maturity that is mixed in with a cheerful ability to get fun out of each day. Paul turned out to be a great member of the family. He is now in nursery school and scoots around skillfully on his special tricycle. Life isn't a bed of roses, but no one should expect that in this world.

In fact, the nursery school teacher said to Liz, "I'm glad Paul is in our class. He has helped the other children accept hard things in their own lives. He is an example to all of us of how happy and creative we can be in spite of our limitations."

Do you believe that people are something special—all people? If so, on what do you base this belief?

And what do you think of the idea that you are special to God?

"In Germany, the Nazis came for the Communists, and I didn't speak up, because I was not a Communist. Then they came for the Jews, and I didn't speak up, because I was not a Jew. . . . Then they came for the Catholics, and I was a Protestant, so I didn't speak up. Then they came for me. . . . By that time, there was no one to speak up for anyone."

Martin Niemöller

Magazines! Now that will be just the thing to cheer up my mother! I thought as I looked at the rows of glossy, beckoning covers.

My mother was ill with exhaustion, and I had the privilege of being able to care for her for two weeks. I wanted her to put her feet up and relax.

This was the first time I had stayed very long in the United States since childhood, and the local shopping center dazed me. Soon I staggered away from the checkout with a pile of magazines propped on top of a bag of groceries.

Later on, my mother and I started leafing through the magazines. Soon we were nearly steaming with anger and frustration—and feeling anything but relaxed.

It wasn't that all of the features we read were wickedly misleading. It was useful to find out a new and better jogging routine and exercises to flatten one's stomach! It was nice to flip past new sewing projects and to read an interesting feature story. But woven into the material were several poisonous points of view. Slowly but surely, they would affect the thinking of anyone who read them.

"This is terrible," one of us would exclaim. "What a mess people would get into if they followed this advice!" Or, "Look at this blatant statement that there is no right and wrong in sex! Think of the people who actually swallow this!"

After a bit I stood up. "I'm sorry, mother! I didn't exactly provide you with reading that would give you peaceful thoughts! I've never seen such a bunch of junk in my life. Why, people might as well read something called *How to Be Your Own Selfish Pig*."

Naturally, we would all like to be happy. We'd like to be satisfied and fulfilled, doing things that we enjoy. From the time we go to kindergarten, we want other people to like and admire us.

> **"I don't care what you say anymore, this is my life! Go ahead with your own life; leave me alone."**
>
> **Billy Joel, "My Life"**

"Let's do something cheap and superficial; Let's do something that we might regret; Let's do something shallow and insensitive, 'Cause this might be the only chance we get."

Sung by Burt Reynolds in *Cannonball Run*

But today it is practically a religion to worship and seek pleasure for oneself. Our culture worships how much "stuff" we amass. It preaches that the career is really our main focus in life. People often sacrifice what they see as life's "little extras" (like family, community, health, or even enjoyment of life) for the furtherance of career or wealth. Our culture also tends to have a fixation on pleasure through sex: the more the better.

Society tells us that we will lose our dignity if we put other people first. One good example is the current attitude that you are being "used" if you sacrifice for or serve others. Be sure not to do the dishes if it's not your turn! If the other person comes back from a hard day feeling grumpy, don't let him flop down while you get his meal and think of ways to make his life easier.

Society and culture tell you that you are meant to be a kind of self-serving pleasure machine. Your highest goal is happiness for yourself. (Why shouldn't it be? Why live for someone else?)

Of course, both my mother and I saw this teaching not just as ideas that were wrong. We had also known lots of people who had tried living like this, and who had experienced unhappiness as a result. We knew the Sallys, the Kathys, the Richards. If there is a right map for human life, it follows that people who go by a faulty map will come to a mighty crash sooner or later.

"But wait a minute," I hear you objecting. "Didn't you just say in the last chapter that people *are* valuable and important? Shouldn't I think of myself that way?"

Yes, you should certainly think of yourself as important. You should realize that humans have tremendous value because they were created by God, with his image stamped in them. God cares about you. He wants you to develop and be all you are meant to be.

But what are you meant to be? That's the big

question. Consider this story of a fish, swimming in a lake. This fish decided he wanted to be free from the boundaries of the lake. He hopped out of the water and landed on the beach. Is he free? He cannot live in the air. His gills flop uselessly.

This is what we are being pressured into doing, as human beings. If we don't live according to the way we were made (according to the principles outlined by our Creator in the Bible), we will soon be in trouble. We enjoy true freedom as human beings when we make the right choices about ourselves and those around us.

It is all very sad. The fish tried to cash in on something extra. In the end, he had nothing but death. And the person who lives for self soon finds his life a nightmare. The body, so pampered and worshiped and served, gets old. The lover leaves. The car rusts. The career fails, or goes sour. The party is over.

The Bible says that we are not the center of the universe, so we should not worship ourselves. God is the highest being, the beginning and the end. We are made to worship and please him—and we're out of line when we don't.

What is a life pleasing to God? Jesus said, "In everything, do to others what you would have them do to you" (Matthew 7:12). This means that, in marriage, you think of what would be nice for your partner in such areas as food, activities, and sexual satisfaction. It means accepting the handicapped person the way you would like to be accepted if you found yourself in a wheelchair.

The same is true of treatment of an old person. How do you want to be treated in a number of years? Or what if you were a kid in an urban ghetto? Wouldn't you like somebody to help you learn to read, let you play in a band, really care about giving you a chance?

If the Bible is true, then this is our proper environment, as water is to a fish. God's ways honestly do work best. They work out best for our own personal good and for the

good of the human race. What a difference it makes to have directions so that we can aim at what is right and what is important. And we can know that, when we fail, God forgives us.

Sally found this. Her search for self-fulfillment had been something that destroyed even her desire to live. Now, she had come to believe in the God who said, "Sally, I love you. You can relax now. The Lord, Christ himself, has taken the guilt of your actions. He will throw away the old record, and give you a new page. You matter. I want you to be loved and happy now and forever. I will show you how I meant you to live."

After experiences like Sally had, healing takes a long time. There are new patterns to choose, all sorts of new ways of treating oneself as well as other people. It helped her to be helping us out in the practical chores of running the extended family that is L'Abri. If you have a glittery, glamorous picture of this old manor house, then please get rid of it! For it was ordinary reality that reassured and helped Sally.

A realistic, biblical picture of life does not show a perfect world. It means that you expect good and not-so-good things in yourself and other people. You don't have to pretend that you are never tired and grouchy or depressed. You don't have to act as if it is always satisfying to clean up after a meal!

Sally happens to be happily married now, with two small children. She is back home in Canada, and we get occasional letters from her. She is not scared of being a "slave" to her family and friends. She is loved, and manages to work at the problems and bad times she hits.

"I still get depressed sometimes," she wrote to me, "but I have learned, in a funny way, not to let that get me down. Anyway, it really is hard to wallow in it for too long. My kids soon drag me back into the sunshine again. The Lord has truly been my light and salvation."

Sadly, not everyone has as clear a grasp of God's purpose for humans as Sally does. Even Christian people whose brains admit that God is there, and who act out a religious life, can fail to put into practice what the Bible says about living. They start acting as if the media's values were right. They, too, get caught up in the web.

Take Penny, for example. Her mother and father were respected church leaders. People admired what they could see of the family—from the outside. But Penny drifted into parties, drinking, and sex. At first it all seemed fun and exciting. But one morning Penny woke up from a hangover and realized that she was pregnant.

When Penny tearfully approached her parents, their big concern was that nobody should find out. Without talking over the huge choice involved, these people left their already distressed daughter with an additional legacy of sadness. They literally railroaded her into an abortion. It was like sweeping ugly dust under the carpet. Now, nobody could think less of them as Christian parents. Everybody could dress up and pretend religion again.

Penny was sent on a European trip: an empty, confused, and unhappy girl. By the mercy of the God who cares, Penny found her way to L'Abri, where she could figure herself out, think about truth, find an answer to her guilt, and learn how to enjoy life again.

Then there was Bob. His missionary parents surely knew the truth of the Bible. But why did they neglect their three children so that their interesting missionary work could take first place?

A bitter, resentful teenaged Bob said to me, "If only I had been somebody else's child, my dad would have had plenty of time for me. But as it was, the only thing I remember was his scolding and rules. I remember the Christmas when I was ten. My aunt sent me a fishing rod. I eagerly asked dad if he would go fishing with me. 'Not this week,' he answered. 'There are a lot of extra meetings at Christmastime.' Well, we never did go fishing together!"

Even though Bob's parents may not have

"**Countless acts by millions of self-centered, instead of God-centered, individuals may reasonably be thought to be destroying the world.**"

G. K. Chesterton

understood what they were doing, they had absorbed the world's value system, which said that one's career is more important than the people in life.

It's easy to absorb wrong values. I think of the typical person's life, and wonder how anyone can grow up with a clear-thinking mind. The average young person is blitzed for hundreds of hours on end by a brain-dulling device: the tv. What is his or her picture of "real life" as it flicks across the screen? Every five minutes advertisements try to get more out of his pocket. Any appeal is used: his desire for popularity, a glamorous sex life, fun, affluence, approval. The watching victim then is treated to a diet of often low-grade entertainment.

Our typical person then leaves the tv set and turns on his radio. Loudly, words are repeated over and over again. What are they saying? What world view is getting across? By now I'm sure you know.

It may be that, as you read this, you realize self-centeredness isn't right. But it's all around you. You may feel afraid that when the crunch comes you'd end up putting

How to Be Your Own Selfish Pig: A Morning Routine

1. **Get up early enough to spend several hours on your personal appearance. First, get dressed. Each of your visible items of clothing should display either a designer label or a small alligator.**

2. **Use whatever cover-up is necessary to make your complexion look perfect. If possible, spread skin with latex paint, since it usually comes with a one-coat-covers-anything guarantee, and also peels off easily at night.**

3. **While applying cover-up, look in the mirror and practice several key lines: "I gotta be me." "This doesn't meet my needs right now." "Hey, give me a little space!" "I can't**

yourself first. After all, the whole world system is set up for us each to live for ourselves. The 1970s and 1980s have been dubbed the "Me Generation."

What can you do if you want to stand against the stream and live as God designed you to?

Read the Bible. Try the Gospels or the letters of Paul. Think about how the Bible presents a completely different idea about living. If it is true, it is a revolution. And it isn't just about keeping rules and "being good." It is honestly exciting to be a fish back in the water! It is good to be a human being accepting the responsibilities and reality of the real world. By comparison the media world is a desert!

You can also pray. Because God is as real as this book, and because he cares about you, you can talk to him just as if he were sitting next to you. You can tell him your concerns and ask for his help.

I have, on many occasions. As you can imagine, with all the people that pass through the L'Abri doors, some are not so easy for me to love. And sometimes I get tired and crabby,

help it; that's just the way I am."

4. **Eat breakfast. Include one-half cup mouthwash as dessert.**

5. **Grab your books and rush out the door. As you walk to school or the bus stop, map out the kind of day you'll enjoy, and avoid whoever or whatever would spoil it. Make a mental list of whom to say hello to and whom to ignore. Don't think about other people's needs and feelings—that causes wrinkles in the forehead.**

6. **If you're ever at a loss for words to express your superiority over other human beings, simply apply the tip of your index finger to the tip of your nose and push upward gently.**

as my family and friends know well. So I ask God to help me love others, even though they don't always fit into my personal "pursuit of happiness"! He answers: sometimes with an idea to rearrange my work schedule so I'm less crabby, or sometimes with an extra dose of love for someone.

Who likes a selfish pig for a friend or loved one? If I always try to satisfy and serve myself, that is exactly what I'll be. But if I am trying to follow the directions for living given by the Creator, it will make a difference in what I do.

Can you sense what your purpose in life should be? If you want to look out for someone besides yourself, you'll need help. Fortunately, God isn't selfish. He wants to look out for you.

"Your real, new self (which is Christ's and also yours, and yours just because it is His) will not come as long as you are looking for it. It will come when you are looking for Him."

C. S. Lewis, *Mere Christianity*

One day at L'Abri Kathy had come out to the vegetable garden with me. We were planning to pick enough beans to feed thirty people, plus some more for freezing. We worked a bit slowly, enjoying the fresh air and the quiet time to talk together.

"These bean plants were weak and scrawny when I came here," Kathy commented. "Now they are so fruitful. I hope I've done as well as they have! I hope all the thinking and finding I've done will result in the right kind of life for me.

"Ever since my parents got divorced, I've been worried about marriage. I know that God planned for people to stick together until death separates them. But how does it work in real life? I've known people, even Christian people, who said it couldn't work for them.

"I'm worried that I'll have a harder time than average getting and staying married. You see, I have lots of sexual memories that are hard to forget. I don't want my life to end up like this." Kathy kicked a yellow, dying bean plant.

"Well, first of all," I said, "you should spend time growing. It will take you time to build up new habits for living. But you aren't alone in this challenge. God will always hear you when you talk to him. And the Holy Spirit has been given to you as a teacher to help you understand the Bible.

"Pray that, in God's own time, he will provide you with the right person to love, if that is his will. Some people are 'in the right place' as singles. But if you are to marry, it will be very important to make a careful choice. Is the person a believer and doer of God's Word? God says this is basic. Spend time really getting to know the person. Find out who he actually is, not who you would like him to be. Could you live with his faults? Don't think that these will disappear! Talk it over with people whom you trust.

"Kathy, I think lots of people throw up their

hands in despair because they expect life to be perfect. When it isn't, they want out. Well, soon they end up with nothing."

I remembered an incident to tell her that had helped me. "One day when I was in kindergarten, a painting of mine was 'ruined' by a red blob of paint. I had angrily prepared to throw it away when my mother stepped in. 'Susan, look, you didn't plan to have a red blob on your painting. But don't throw the whole thing out! You worked hard on it. Now, let's see.' She urged me to use that red paint in the picture.

"In the same way, Kathy, you'll find problems in both single life and marriage. Don't walk out right away and pursue happiness for yourself. Look for ways of going on in spite of problems. I know a couple whose dream was to build their own lakeside cabin. But the wife was disabled in a car crash. They had to use their money in other ways.

"In some aspects, the husband now had a different wife from the one he had married. He could have quit. But he didn't. It was hard work, but they are now living happy lives. Every life, single or married, has hard things in it. We always get a paint-splattered picture to work with!"

Kathy thoughtfully picked up a basket, now brimming over with beans. "My friends will think I'm crazy and old-fashioned sticking to the Bible's rules. But now I'm sure which ideas work in life."

I straightened up with my basket on my arm, and we walked away from the garden. "For me," I said, "it's been exciting, challenging, fun, and interesting to serve my family and other people! Somebody should spend a billion dollars advertising the joys and rewards of this responsibility."

Kathy laughed, set down her basket, and pretended she was on television. "Be a wife, a husband, a father, a mother, a loving sister or uncle. Care for someone else. Be human. Try it—you'll like it!"

One rainy November day, I was relaxing in front of the fireplace in our family room with my little baby, Ranald John, nestled in my arms. I love peaceful moments like this. The warm baby dozed as the rain hissed against the windows.

Kim, a new student at L'Abri, had come up to meet me, and she sat on the other side of the fire. After chatting a bit, she suddenly asked, "That is your fourth baby, isn't it?"

"Yes," I answered, "it is."

"I can see that all your children seem happy, and that you and your husband enjoy them. But you know, they can't always live safely here in an English country garden! I don't see how you can bear to think of bringing children into such a terrible and meaningless world!"

Kim wasn't being impolite. She was asking a good question. A little baby. We hold it and ask, "What is human life all about? Can we find the key to its meaning? What is there that makes life worth living?"

One good way to find out what people think life is all about is to ask them the question, "How would you spend tomorrow if you knew it was your last day?"

Some people would try to do something on the last day of their lives to become famous. We all want some part of us to endure forever.

Frighteningly, several assassins have mentioned similar motives for killing their famous victims. "They can gas me, but I am famous. I have achieved in one day what it took Robert Kennedy all his life to do," said Sirhan Sirhan after shooting the presidential candidate in 1968.

Others, if they thought tomorrow was their last day of life, would do some good deed. They hope that, though they can't live forever, they can leave the world a better place than when they entered it.

"If man were immortal, do you realize what his meat bills would be?"

Woody Allen, *Getting Even*

The problem with both the hope for fame and the hope for world improvement is that they aren't very sure hopes. The person who tries to be remembered can't be sure he really will be—or for how long. And the person who tries to improve the world does not—unless he believes in the God of the Bible—have any assurance that his efforts will do any good. Scientific research, for example, can be used for good or evil—just as nuclear energy can be put into electric power plants or into neutron bombs. The world might become worse, not better. At least the person tried to help—but does that trying make living worthwhile?

Some people, if you asked how they would spend their last day on earth, would probably tell you they'd throw a party. They feel that the best they can do to make their lives worthwhile is to live for themselves. They go out for maximum enjoyment—to "grab the gusto," as the beer commercial recommends, since "you only go round once in life."

"Is that all there is?" the song asks. "If that's all there is, my friend, then let's keep dancing. Let's break out the booze and have a ball, if that's all there is. . . ."

This song expresses the same desperation Kim felt. What is there that makes life worth living?

"Well, that might be the way I would think," I replied to Kim's honest question, "if I could only look for meaning in what I see. There are beautiful and good things, but also wars, famines, psychological torments, loneliness. If what we can see is all there is, any feeling person might think that this planet isn't a good place for new life! Especially if you think we are just animals, with no ultimate meaning. Why bother?

"But if Christianity is true, then the reality is quite different. This little child is a unique human being. His desires, relationships, and achievements will have meaning. He has directions about how to live that work. Most importantly, he will understand that he is in a universe where the Creator cares for him, even now.

114

"He will grow up knowing that his life will not end at physical death. He will be aware that the final end of the planet isn't nuclear destruction, for the Bible promises that Jesus is actually coming back to earth. Then polluted rivers will run clean and pure again, and the human race will live under a completely fair government. Even the dead will be given new bodies, just as Jesus had, and there won't be any more sickness."

The rain hissed, and the orange flames leaped up in the grate. I hugged my baby, feeling thankful again to God that I could be sure that his message is reliable.

"Why, you actually expect that all of this will happen!" Kim exclaimed. "You are talking about this as if it is going to be as much a part of this child's life as the fact that next year he'll be walking!"

"Yes. Otherwise the whole thing doesn't make sense. And Christianity wouldn't be an answer or a hope. If you really believe something, you expect it to be true. You plan on it."

I told her the story of a scientist who had supposedly invented a cure for cancer. He said that he had a special light you could bask in that would cure you in five and a half days! One day the scientist found that he had cancer in his big toe. But instead of taking off his socks and turning on his special light, he bought a ticket for a large city with a cancer hospital. His actions didn't show that he believed what he had claimed to believe.

Consider a nineteen-year-old boy in a town not far from where we live. He spent his time staring out of the hospital windows. Eric's questions frightened him, because he knew he was dying. But nobody had talked frankly with him about it. The medical staff pretended he was getting better. They had advised the family that it was kinder for Eric not to face the truth. This meant that visits were painful for everybody. The family would chat with forced cheerfulness: nobody feels comfortable lying.

Eric couldn't bring himself to say, "Hey, you guys. Cut the acting. You know I'm dying. I know I'm dying."

Somebody told my husband, Ranald, about Eric. That same day, Ranald visited him. They started talking about God, and some of the reasons we have for knowing that he is actually there. Eric watched the gulls swooping over the newly

Battling the Monsters

Some plane rides across the Atlantic to America have been fun occasions for me. One trip was just the opposite. After I had buckled the seat belt, I plugged in the earphones, turned up the classical music, and prepared myself for eight hours of being alone to struggle with my questions and doubts.

A week or so before, I had heard that my dad had cancer. I had felt stunned, as if I had hit a brick wall while traveling at fifty miles per hour. We didn't know if dad could pull through, because the cancer was advanced. I had to face the possibility of death. This time it was not a pretend mind trip. It was for real.

As I sat there, I realized that mingling with my shock, my sadness, and my fears was something uglier. A wild-eyed monster, drooling at the jaws, was staring at me: fear. *What if it's not all true after all? You haven't been through death and seen that Christianity is true. What if the Bible is an empty hope?*

For a few minutes I wallowed in panic. Then the practical Susan of the Swiss vegetable patch surfaced to help me. *Think it out. Stop letting your emotions scare you out of your wits!*

I forced myself away from thinking about what "might be," and talked to myself. *Why do you think that the Bible's view is truth? Does this key fit the keyhole of reality?*

Mentally, I checked whether the Bible's key fit. *Ah, yes, it explains the order and complexity of the universe. It explains why persons are unique, experiencing love, choice, beauty, right and wrong.*

116

plowed field that was visible from the hospital window. In his slow country accent, he told Ranald he had always known that there was a God. In fact, he said, he used to think about God as he plowed the rich Hampshire fields. "The countryside was so

I thought of the archaeological digs, and the evidence that the Bible is a true history. I thought of the prophecies fulfilled. Then there was the miracle of the unity of the Bible, even though its writing spanned hundreds of years and dozens of people.

In my mind, I bent over the pile of keys that claimed to be possible answers to life. *Ah, here is the key of the Eastern philosophies and religions. Very clever, but it doesn't fit the world the way it is. And here we have the primitive religions. But if I were to climb up Mount Olympus, I would not find the gods feasting there. If I look behind the lightning, there is no thunder god lurking. These myths never fit reality.*

In my mind, I picked up another key. *Of course, this is the key that fits! The Bible is truth, not wishful thinking!*

Peace and calm came to me, and I was able to eat a bit of the dinner the stewardess served. I still cried. I still had fears. But they were very, very different, for under me was solid ground. I knew that God was real, true, reliable. His communication fit into history and reality. I could depend on him.

People often ask me, "Do you really believe all this Christianity stuff?"

And my answer is yes. Of course, I have been tempted to doubt it sometimes, and probably will again. But I can keep coming back to the sureness of it all. It fits and makes sense. When I act on the Lord's promises, they hold true.

God is really there. He has spoken to us. His love for us is too great for words.

Have you found and tried out the key that works?

"On humanist assumptions, life leads to nothing. . . . If there is a bridge over a gorge which spans only half the distance and ends in mid-air, and if the bridge is crowded with human beings pressing on, one after another until they fall into the abyss . . . , it does not matter where they think they are going, what preparations for the journey they may have made, how much they may be enjoying it all."

H. J. Blackham, *Objections to Humanism*

"Often this earth has no time for my feelings, Under His love is where I find my rest. . . . Under His love, He takes away my sorrow. I've found my place, I've no desire to roam. I watch the skies, for He may come back tomorrow, And if He does, well I'm ready to go home."

Steve Camp and Larry Norman, "Under His Love"

beautiful, I knew that God had made it, but I didn't know anything else about him."

Soon they were talking about dying. Eric was relieved simply to share his fears and questions. Ranald explained that death itself is not normal for the human being, that God had not planned for our souls and bodies to be separated by the grave. God will someday overcome both evil and death. This was good news for Eric.

Ranald went to the hospital every day to be with Eric. In those few days, they were able to read some of the wonderful promises God has given in his Word. Ranald was able to tell Eric that there was a sure way to go right to heaven and God after death, through the gift of new, everlasting life the Lord Jesus gives to each one who chooses to say, "Yes, God. I accept your pardon. Thank you for it."

Eric would look out at the winter trees during his last days and listen to the passages of the Bible that have brought comfort to so many thousands of human beings. He particularly liked to hear the words of the Twenty-third Psalm. "Even though I walk through the valley of the shadow of death, I will fear no evil, for you are with me; . . . and I will dwell in the house of the Lord forever" (verses 4, 6).

Surely this is better than the death with soma in *Brave New World.* For death is not the end!

If Christianity is truth, then it is solid and testable. It is like a key that is exactly right. I can therefore trust it, and use it, even in hard times.

The danger today is that we who believe in the God of the Bible often go on living like everybody else—especially if our Christian understanding is wobbly and unsure. We miss out on many benefits the Bible promises to us in this life. We should be bold enough to say, "If the Bible is true, then I can act on what it says."

Of course, nobody can do this all the time. It is easy to keep forgetting that God is actually there, easy to let our minds get foggy. But the Bible encourages us to look afresh at our lives every day. It challenges us to put truth into practice. The little baby, the teenager, the adult, the old person—all of us are completely different when we understand and believe what God has told us.

Go ahead and ask questions: "Who am I? Where am I going? How will I get there? How do I *know*?"

And consider the Bible's answer. For God is there. He is real. He cares about even the sparrow—so think how much more he cares about you!

"I believe in Christianity as I believe the sun has risen, not only because I see it, but because by it I see everything else."

C. S. Lewis

About the Author

Though Susan Schaeffer Macaulay was born in the United States, she has lived in Europe for most of her life. Her parents, Francis and Edith Schaeffer, moved to Switzerland when Susan was only eight years old, in order to help European churches in the wake of World War II. Their ministry took shape as the first L'Abri Fellowship Center when Susan was fourteen, and as a teen she took full part in activities and discussions with people from around the world.

After attending a college of occupational therapy in Oxford, Susan married Ranald Macaulay, a Cambridge law student (and theology graduate from King's College, London) whom she had met at L'Abri. Together they began the British branch of L'Abri, first in London, and currently in Greatham.

The mother of four children, Susan enjoys writing when she can find the time in and around her L'Abri work. She is the author of a children's book, *Something Beautiful from God*.

About the Artist

Slug Signorino had a strong interest in art even in kindergarten, he remembers, and he pursued that interest throughout his schooling. Now he works in illustration full-time from his studio in Michigan City, Indiana, where his two dogs and two cats keep him company. His humorous drawings have appeared in Scholastic magazines and books, in periodicals like *Seventeen, Supermag, Chicago,* and *Outside,* on posters for the Museum of Contemporary Art in Chicago, and more. Slug's wife is also an artist, and three of their four children are studying art.